faces of hastings

faces of hastings

Diversity in a Rural Nebraska Community

 Hastings College Press | Hastings, Nebraska

© 2019 by Hastings College Press

All rights reserved. No part of this book may be used or reproduced in any manner whatsoever without permission from the publisher, except in the case of brief quotations embodied in critical articles and reviews.

The views and opinions expressed in this book are those of the interviewees and do not necessarily reflect official policy or views of Hastings College or Hastings College Press.

Copy Editors
Lyette Erin   Abigail Shaw

Proofreaders
Davianne Czarnick   Jenny Sells

Designer
Patricia Oman

ISBN-10: 1942885660
ISBN-13: 978-1-942885-66-5

Manufactured in the United States of America.

contents

brandi bosier   1

julie clawson   13

adolfo diaz-vargas   27

chad dumas and dawn vincent dumas   33

delta fajardo-norton   53

lanae hall   67

xyeria hayes   73

jose jimenez   83

ann koozer   101

chris langenberg   111

raquel maar   121

carlos (gus) magallanes   131

julie mcdougal   137

casey molifua   143

june mueller   153

tamisha osgood   159

melissa pedroza   167

wayne perez   179

sam and elizabeth (ella) rathod   193

ellis riley   203

sabrina rodriguez   217

ralph southern   227

josefa (bee) thomas   237

scott thomsen   257

siying (stella) wu   271

zaid   283

introduction

Faces of Hastings celebrates difference and diversity in a small town at the heart of America—Hastings, Nebraska. Located at the intersection of Pawnee footpaths, the old Oregon Trail, Interstate-80, and the millenia-old north-south skyway for migrating cranes, Hastings is a vibrant and multi-faceted community.

This project began in the fall of 2018, when a group of Hastings College students and professors collaborated with community members to document the diversity of Hastings through a series of oral history interviews. Students from three different classes—Dr. Jessica Henry's Intercultural Communication class, Dr. Jean Heriot's Cultural Anthropology class, and Dr. Constance Malloy's Literature of North American Diversity class—conducted interviews with thirty-six Hastings residents in the fall of 2018. After completing the interviews, students transcribed the audio to create coherent stories of each participant's life. In the winter and spring of 2019, students from Dr. Patricia Oman's Book Production class, Prof. Sara Gevurtz's Introduction to Graphic Design class, and Dr. Pedro

Vizoso's Spanish Translation class collaborated to edit, translate, and present the interviews in a public exhibit at the Adams County Historical Society and the book currently in your hands.

This project is modeled after the 2003 *Faces of Change* project in Pelican Rapids, Minnesota. The small community of around 2,500 residents was becoming increasingly diverse as more and more immigrants moved to town to work in the turkey processing plant. The library director, Pam Westby, wanted to introduce the residents of Pelican Rapids to each other and to "bridge the chasm created by language and culture."[1] The initial stage of the process was a photo-documentary exhibit at the public library. The second stage of the process was a book titled *Faces of Change*.

The Interviews

Though there are many ways to define diversity, students were instructed to think of diversity in broad terms: race and ethnicity, gender and sexuality, immigration status, religion, socio-economic status, employment, political beliefs, age, single and partnered parents, and homelessness. Students selected persons to interview from their own connections or sought guidance from their professors.

The content of the interviews in this book is recorded in the words of the participants. Changes were made only to improve the readability of the story (for example, deleting thought run-ons or organizing the information more clearly). Any information that was added by the interviewers is placed in brackets.

History of Hastings

The interviews in this book reveal a continuous, layered history of displacement, immigration, and settlement in the Hastings area. Although well-established by now, the town continues to evolve. *Faces of Hastings* is a snapshot of one moment in the town's history.

Prior to Euro-American settlement, this large area of the prairie near the Platte River was part of the territory of the Pawnee, a Plains tribe generally considered to be friendly to settlers. Treaties were negotiated in 1833, 1848, and 1857; in 1857 the Pawnee were moved to Oklahoma by agents of the US government, opening up this territory for more Euro-American settlers.[2]

In the 19th century, the area in central Nebraska surrounding Hastings was referred to as the Great American Desert because of the scarcity of trees, rivers, and lakes.[3] Even so, settlers who were encouraged by the Homestead Act of 1863 started to take notice of the flat and fertile land of Adams County. By the mid-1800s, the area around Hastings was being scouted as a stop for the railroad, and in 1872 the first railroad, the Burlington and Missouri River Railroad, reached Hastings. In fact, Hastings was founded by, and named for, Colonel Thomas D. Hastings, a contractor for the St. Joseph and Denver City Railroad. By 1874 Hastings became an incorporated city.[4] To attract more residents, in 1879 the railroads published brochures that described Adams County as "healthful—capable of curing most known ailments; fertile, with well-drained farmland suited to the production of orchards, tobacco, and other farm crops."[5] At the time of the 1870 census, there were only nineteen residents in Adams County, but only ten years later there were 8,609 residents.[6]

The first white settlers into the Hastings area were mostly native-born Americans, but soon immigrants started arriving from England, Ireland, Germany, Austria, Russia, Denmark, and other countries. Although many of them came to the area for the chance to own land and farm, others came for jobs in the developing industries. Starting in the late 1800s, four brickyards operated in Hastings, producing 70% of all brick made in Nebraska and 100% of the paving bricks for the state. The other big industry in Hastings just after the turn of the century was cigar manufacturing. John Kipp founded the Kipp Cigar Company in 1909, and it produced 10 million hand-rolled cigars annually. Most of the workers for both industries were Germans from Russia who had migrated from Germany to Russia in the 1760s and then to America beginning in the 1870s.[7]

The population of Hastings exploded after the construction of the Naval Ammunition Depot in 1942. This was the largest Navy Ammunition plant during World War II, and it employed 10,000 people before closing in 1966.[8] Today there are still many major manufacturers in Hastings, including Dutton Lainson, Thermo King, and T-L Irrigation, to name a few. The largest employer in Hastings is Mary Lanning Hospital, which opened in 1915. In addition, Hastings continues to be a hub for higher education, with both Hastings College and Central Community College making their homes in Hastings.

In 2019 Hastings has a population of just under 25,000 people. The real claim to fame for this small midwestern town is as the birthplace of Kool-Aid, invented by Edwin Perkins in the 1920s.[9] Although the population is predominately white (84.8%) and most are US citizens (95.6%), the city does have a vibrant infusion of diversity. There is a significant Hispanic community (11%), as well as smaller communities of Asian residents (1.5%), and Black residents (.94%). The median property value in Hastings is $103,800, and the median household income is $46,903.

Even so, there is still a fairly high number of residents living below the poverty level (12.5%).[10] The majority of the residents in Hastings are Christian (57.7% in Adams County),[11] but there are smaller pockets of the population who are Jewish, Baha'i, Muslim, or other religions, and many who are either atheists or non-practicing.

Acknowledgments

We would like to acknowledge all those who contributed to this project. Hastings College professors Dr. Jessica Henry (project coordinator), Dr. Jean Heriot, Dr. Constance Malloy, Dr. Patricia Oman, Dr. Pedro Vizoso, and Prof. Sara Gevurtz all worked to make this project an interdisciplinary effort. The following students worked hard to make this project come alive:

- *Interviews:* Bailly Ballard, Cornelius Barber, Jenny Borge, Kaelan Dae, Michelle DeCoud, Jeremiah De Irish, Joelle Derner, Stratton Discoe, Paul Erickson, Erick Espinoza, Adam Fitzgerald, Collin Fowler, Ryder Ghidotti, Elizabeth Hansen, Alex Hartwick, Timothy Herbek, Walker Hermann, Alex Holmes, Brennin Leach, Ben LeBar, Kaeden Markham, Marcus Medcalf, Josh Merithew, Abigail Olson, AJ Osborn,

David Panter, Andie Paschal, Basil Rabayda, Alex Rieflin, Gabi Rodgers, Veronica Schermerhorn, Tyler Schoen, Jenny Sells, Jeff Sokol, Jess Trad, and Mackenzie Waltemath.
- *Editing, Organization, and Proofreading:* Lyette Erin, Abigail Shaw, Davianne Czarnick, and Jenny Sells.
- *Portraits and Exhibit Design:* Austin Bretting, Dariana Burr, Carter Mason, Max Moreno, Caitlin Pilapil, Danielle Shenk, Caitlin Smith, Austin Uhlig, Megan Vaughn.
- *Translation:* Celeste Borg, Sarah Barger, Ashley Caudill, Leo Perez, Jorge Lopez Cereijo, Victor Moreno Requena, Abby Morillon.

Sandy Sypherd (Hastings Multicultural Association), Carlos Barcenas and Margaret Marsh (Center for Rural Affairs), and the YWCA of Adams County helped us to solicit interview participants. Elizabeth Spillinek (Adams County Historical Society/Oral History Initiative) lent us audio recorders, and we gathered much of the information about Hastings from the publications of the ACHS. The staff at the Hastings Museum, including Becky Matticks, agreed to help us turn our project into a museum display, giving us the space to make the *Faces of Hastings* even more visible.

Grant funding for *Faces of Hastings* was provided by the Hastings Community Foundation.

And, finally, we want to thank all of the people of Hastings who were willing to let their faces serve as examples of our vibrant and diverse community.

Notes

1. Jarvis Ellison, J. (2007). *The Faces of Change.* Ottertail County Historical Society. Fergus Falls, MN.
2. Hyde, G. E. (1988). *The Pawnee Indians* (Revised Edition). Norman, OK: University of Oklahoma Press.
3. *Adams County Nebraska: Nebraska Historic Buildings Survey* (1999). Prepared for the Nebraska State Historical Society State Preservation Office, city of Hastings, Adams County, and Adams County Historical Society.
4. "About Hastings History." *Adams County Historical Society Historical News* Vol. 25 No. 4, and Vol. 27 No. 4.
5. Weyer Creigh, D. (1972). *Adams County: The Story 1872-1972.* Adams County-Hastings Centennial Commission.
6. Ibid.

7. Spilinek, E. (2007). *Fountain to Fountain Walking Tour Brochure.* Adams County Historical Society.
8. "The Naval Ammunition Depot." *Adams County Historical Society Historical News* Vol. 25 No. 4 and Vol. 27 No. 4.
9. *History of Kook-Aid* (2002). Adams County Historical Society. http://kool-aiddays.com/history/
10. U.S. Census Bureau statistics (2014) compiled by DataUSA for Hastings, NE. https://datausa.io/profile/geo/hastings-ne/
11. Grammich, C., Hadaway, K., Houseal, R., Jones, D. E., Krindatch, A., Stanley, R., & Taylor, R.H. (2012). *2010 U.S. Religion Census: Religious Congregations & Membership Study.* Association of Statisticians of American Religious Bodies. Jones, Dale E., et al. 2002. Congregations and Membership in the United States 2000. Nashville, TN: Glenmary Research Center.

brandi bosier

Interviewed by David Panter

I am an artist. I created the Hastings College Christmas light display. I also take care of the city Christmas lights downtown [that you see] on the rooftops. I also have my art car. It sits in an old garage. Nobody knows what's in there. In 2017, I won the national art car championship. Art cars from all over the country, 120 of us, including two from Canada, went to Colorado. We won the award there. They personally make it. Ronnie Wood is the curator of the art car show down there. His work has been opened in New York, his paintings and so forth. Hastings has a lot of culture and art in it, and I'm proud of that.

My kids and my grandkids keep me here. In 1997, I became the first trans woman to win custody of my children in Adams County. It was very expensive. In two years, my home [was checked], and they said that I was the best parent. I'm glad to say that my kids are doing well. They struggle like every other middle- or low-income [person]. You really have no middle-income left. Politically, I'm really involved. I'm the first trans woman to be an elected delegate from the state of Nebraska to go to the Democratic National Convention in Philadelphia in 2016. I was asked to be interviewed by several national publications, TV and radio, at that convention. I spent my time doing things that might further what we can make happen for LGBT rights, human rights, women's rights, and gun rights.

Advocacy is big on my list. I have backed off quite a bit during the current administration because all we're doing right now is trying to save face and not lose any ground. Marriage equality has been attacked on several different issues. We're waiting for national marriage equality to be attacked. Next month, there's a court case coming up for the Supreme Court which is going to eliminate the ability for state attorneys to attack people who have been pardoned on presidential pardon. This is scary. Nobody knows. We're all thinking it's about the #MeToo movement. It's like when we started attacking immigrants coming into the country and we were protesting [at] airports. Meanwhile, they were at the federal level taking away social security. That's money that we paid into, and they were taking money out of that while we were being blindfolded. It's happening. We just see more of it because it's more open and there's more people involved now.

I hate organized religion and what it's become. There is no "Make America Great Again." That isn't going to happen. We're not going to

KKK slavery and all the other crap that they want. We've just taken slavery to a different level. Now we use money to make our slaves happy. That's just the dynamics of our social environment we live in today. If you examine religion and you look back at 300 AD, the Apostles' Creed was not the apostle's creation. There were twelve tribes down the Mediterranean, and they came together, and they decided to say, "Don't commit this. Don't do that." That's where the Apostles' Creed came from. It was renamed that later. In the sixteenth century, King James tried to interpret the Bible, and they picked and chose what they wanted to. So, I don't have a lot of use for [the Bible], but there are a lot of good things in there that need to be paid attention to.

As for the spirituality part, you have a conscience, and you feel bad when you do something to somebody, or you feel good when you do something to somebody. That's your spirituality. We are spiritual beings, and we are all connected spiritually. As far as spirit, I believe I'm of a healthy spirit. I have a lot of friends. I also, as a trans woman, do the tree care for the Catholic Church in town. I've been able to break boundaries there. That's probably the hardest one that you're going to break for the LGBT community. As far as religion, and I will tell them right to their face, "Which part of your book do you want to use today?" I look at religion as a book. Spirituality, it's everything to us as human beings. The ultimate, supreme commandment in that book is love one another as yourself ... and remember, you're not the head cheese. If everybody could do that, my goodness, we'd have such a great world.

[Concerning] my life here, I own a business. I also do tree care. The only arboretum here is [at] Hastings College. I used to do the tree care there for fifteen, twenty years. Our county extension agent, who is supposed to be our top person to go to for arbor culture, horticulture, I do his trees at his house. I own three bucket trucks, all sorts of equipment, and I do an awful lot of tree care. That's my life here in Hastings. I was willing to sell and move away from everything back in the early 2000s when I transitioned, if that's what it took. I would move to the land of acceptance, California, if I had to.

I was born in Hollywood on Sunset Boulevard. We moved back here when I was two years old. My youngest daughter was born in Twin Falls, Idaho in 1988. We moved out to Idaho from 1986 to 1990. [I have] my kids, my grandkids, my foster kids, and adoptive kids.

I went through a divorce, and it wasn't because of who I was. I was out to my partner before I got married, but we had other issues involved. So, we went our separate ways. My current relationship is with my hubby. My partner runs all over the country taking hurt dogs in on a volunteer basis. My current relationship is run healthy. As long as my hubby makes sure that the garbage is out, I'm good. My partner is also a trans person. I knew that going into the relationship, and we enjoy a really great relationship. We've got one kid through that relationship. That is successfully working. She's eighteen years old.

In kindergarten, I got straight A's. Because I was so feminine in high school, I received a lot of bullying issues. In tenth grade, I was doing twelfth-grade algebra and getting paid for it because I needed money for other things. I was getting paid do other people's homework. I quit in my twelfth-grade year, but I've been back twice for auto mechanics career day by the same instructor, Tim Smith. It isn't that I didn't want to be there. I just wasn't gonna put up with the b.s. I want to get on with my life and start moving forward. That was in 1982. In 1984, I went back and got my certificate of our arbor culture. I've been doing arbor culture my whole life. I've also worked at other jobs while I built my business. I studied business and management in 1984 and 1985 at Central Community College and received my associate's [degree] in that. The problem is this: life is too short. That's where my issues came into play, how I'd make decisions. I've continued my education in different areas. I don't think there's a whole lot that has intrigued me that I haven't looked into or taking courses on.

I'm an engineer because that's how my mind thinks, engineering. I do an awful lot as far as fabricating and fixing. I own my own shop and other land properties here in town. I just had a 1956 International truck in my shop. When this guy had problems, because it's an old 5060, he couldn't find the right parts. I had to engineer and make this truck work again. It's a lift truck that you can go up on and do work on.

Some of us have had a very, very overwhelming drag career. I'm a fire breather. I do all sorts of stuff on stage. I have a lot of fun with that. I've since retired from all that. I won Nashville Promoter of the Year two years in a row, lots of other accolades along the way, and lots of crowns. After I became an icon, and I was paid to perform in Las Vegas, I said, "That's enough for me." It's time to just enjoy my kids, my grandkids, my life. I got heavy back into races this year. We have a lot of fun.

I joined drag because it was an art. It allowed me to express myself. I've never made any money because I've always donated it back. When I was [in my] early twenties, I started going down to Kansas City to a club called Missy B's. They would have open mic night. You get discovered by queens that have been doing it for a time. Eventually you start getting invited into shows. It's just like any other career as far as the entertainment field. You have to pay attention to who's doing the drugs on the floor. You gotta stay away from the sex work and so forth.

I am clean. I've lived a great life. I've never had an issue with anything. I've stayed out of all that. Not that I don't mind going to Colorado every now and then but that's just beside the point. I think that there's some issues that we really need to examine. I mean, Einstein loved acid, so what the hell.

I have performed all over the country, and I'm very grateful for that. I've had the chance to experience a lot of different other cities from the LGBT side, which is one of the most attacked social subcultures. Hastings is a "you respect me, I respect you" town. That's the words that I've used for the last ten years. You respect me, I respect you. That's what it is. That means we're going to be friendly, and we're going to enjoy each other's company. We're gonna do business. We're gonna do whatever. If we want to say something, we're going to say it to your face.

What's your primary hand for writing? Which is your dominant hand? How did you know that? It was the hand the pen was put in when you were younger, and you just left it that way. That's kind of like gender. Which hand is your dominant hand? Which gender is yours? That's what I've instilled in Hastings. I've been living my life for a long time here. I've done a lot of shows here in town to bring the LGBT culture [to] the people. I believe that that's really conquered a lot of barriers. I'm at the point where I'm scared to tell my LGBT friends how good

Hastings is because I'm scared they'll all come here. It only takes one [bad] apple to ruin it.

Somebody asked me which businesses in Hastings are friendly to LGBT. There aren't any negative businesses. There's negative business experiences, but you're going to see that in any situation. There are a few people that have issues, and they're open about it. But guess what? That's what we need to be so we can look at them, examine them, and look past them.

[There's] nothing significant that stands out [for times I was discriminated against in Hastings]. I have lost bids because of who I am, one or two at the most. It really is minimal at best. Hastings has had a really good track record. There's been a lot of great leadership for the community. The GSA has been present. I've been part of the Alliance for Hastings College. There has been a lot of great leadership in Hastings. For me to come along when I did really bridged a gap between then and now. That really helped Hastings move forward. I wish other cities could do and see that. Hastings doesn't seem like it, but it's a really educated town, very culturally accepting. I'll say that there really isn't a lot of issues.

[However,] the patriarchy runs the show. I can name five wealthy people that tell the city council what to do and what not to do. You're going to find a lot of that because change doesn't happen overnight. We're getting there, but change doesn't happen overnight. To give you an example, our present mayor; very astute, nice guy, well educated; spent $38,000 getting a job to pay $6,000 a year. [He spent] $38,000 on his campaign. That's open public [knowledge]; that isn't hidden behind us. That's just open [to the] public. Hastings is a town that's been run by people that [have money]. If you're an outsider, you're going to be allowed to live, be comfortable, and enjoy culture and Hastings for what it is. You're not going to advance business-wise in Hastings unless you become part of or are accepted by the [main people]. A lot of places [are like that].

Hastings is really above and beyond most communities [when it comes to] being accepting. As far as a business community, there are a lot of improvements we can make. We've fallen behind. Towns, such as Grand Island, used to be the same size as Hastings. Now they're twice the population. Granted, they're closer to the interstate. Demographics play a big part in this, but there are things we've fallen behind in too. We have not allowed some businesses to excel. The city is very guarded on some of the bigger contracts. That's something that I'd like to see opened up more. I'd like to see more business opportunities for the culturally diverse people to come to Hastings. That's something [that's] really important.

[In the community, I looked up to] Hal Lainson. They own quite a few of the industries in Hastings. Hal Lainson was a multimillionaire. [He] was the kind of person that even if he was completely broke, he would have been the nicest person I ever met. There were twelve or thirteen of us associates, as he liked to call us. I take care of all the tree care there and you'll notice the cottonwoods are almost 100 years old there. They're huge. He was planting more trees in Hastings than anybody else. All of the trees on University Avenue he planted. He paid for all that. He really was an admiral in business in Hastings. At his funeral, he had us twelve associates, that took care of stuff at his property, go with the family. Then we walked out behind the family and sat in the pew right behind them. Every person in Hastings was there, and we were treated so respectfully. If there was ever an issue, you went to Hal, and he would find help or help you through it.

The man passed away at [age] ninety-eight in the best way. His last three to five years of life, whenever I was over [at his house], he would usually call me up to his room around two o'clock in the afternoon. He was pretty much bedridden upstairs in his mansion. He would give a lot of advice. I had the opportunity to have Professor Lance, as I liked to call him, teach me business ethics for quite a long time on a personal level, one-on-one. Can you imagine that experience? He was my hero in Hastings as far as business.

As far as LGBT human rights activists, [that would be] my trans mother, Dana. She passed away in January. She would go around to corporate primary companies and give the trans one-on-one speech, a speech I now give. She was really big. She was part of the fourteen people that sat down in Dallas, Texas when a senator said, "What do we refer to you gender different people as?" They came up with the word *transgender* back in 1996. She was from Hastings. Her daughter, Laura, has got a degree here from Hastings too. She now lives in Hawaii. That would be my human rights activist hero here in Hastings.

I've been able to draw from quite a bit of really great humanists. Let's keep it in perspective. They're not gods, but they're great leadership.

My husband and I moved here in 2002 with our two young daughters, who were two and four years old at the time. He was offered a job. It was shortly after September 11th happened. We moved here from the East Coast, [where] we were very close to that event. [We thought,] what better a place to raise two little girls than in the middle of Nebraska? When we came out to visit before my husband accepted the job, he came for an interview. I remember walking down Second Street. People looked us in the eye and they said, "Good morning!" That actually put us off a little. It was a little disarming. I said to my husband, "Don't look back, they'll want us to join a church or something. Just keep looking straight ahead." It was just very strange that people looked you in the eye, and they said, "Good morning," and they meant it. So, we sort of packed up our two kids, our pug, a couple of birds and we headed west on I-80.

Life was a lot slower. We joked. We called it the Nebraska project. We thought we would be here for three years, because my husband was just coming off a

Interviewed by Marcus Medcalf

julie clawson

postdoc. We thought, "Well, this will be his first job after his PhD, and we'll get our feet wet." He'll do the science. I'll raise the babies. We're still here. Our kids are in college now.

I was born in Boston. My father was a pretty religious Jewish man. My mother [was] not as religious. I was brought up in a very traditional Jewish home. I went to Hebrew school. [I] got suspended from Hebrew school, because I suggested that maybe the Palestinians had a point. It was 1973. I wanted to know where they went when Israel got their country, and I got in trouble. I was eight. When I was fifteen, my father passed away. I questioned my religion. I questioned everything, because my father was a healthy man. He was a good man. You learn in your faith [that] God protects what is good. I was like, "What's this?" So, I rebelled and questioned everything. Then I went off to college, and when you go off to college, you spread your wings and you learn about all different kinds of cultures. I went away, and I lived with a young woman from Thailand who was Buddhist. That was the coolest thing ever. She was actually part of the very upper class from Thailand. So, I learned how the rich Thai people lived and that was a whole other cultural experience, because she had no idea there were oppressed people in Thailand. I was very politically active, so we had to educate.

My parents were born here. My grandparents were not. My grandmother was a product of the Russian Revolution. Her story was when she was about six, which would have been 1917, her family was killed, and she walked to Poland. I don't know with whom she walked to Poland. The story got a little convoluted as we grew up, but she made her way to Poland. [She] lived with a Christian family who helped her get to the United States. She landed in Boston as a teenager and met my grandfather, who was born in Russia also. [He] had come over, but they didn't come over together. They got married. They had a little store in Boston, and that's where my father was born. My mother's parents ... my Nana was born in Romania. She came to Boston, also somewhere in the Bolshevik Revolution. Her story's a little shady to us too. I don't know a whole lot about my mother's father, because he died when she was young. So, I am a second generation American.

Very much at the forefront of the Jewish culture is education, mostly because of the Jews being persecuted for so many years. To be educated is to have power. Especially since the Holocaust, the Jews were powerless. Education was always so important. My father put himself through college. He went to Northeastern University. My mother didn't finish college until I was in the second grade. She was one of the first women to graduate [from] her program in mechanical engineering.

In the 1970s, that was a big deal for a woman. My father died before I graduated high school, and they were very serious about education. They thought it would be a good idea if I went into medicine. I thought that would be a good career choice too. Except, I was a really talented musician, and I got a scholarship to the Hartt Conservatory of Music. I wanted to be an opera singer. My father would have turned over in his grave, but my mother was like, "What am I going to do? You're seventeen and you're winning things." So, I went to Hartt.

I got two degrees in opera. I sang for a living, but I met my husband. [I] love my husband. I wanted to have a dog and a host plant. So, I toured for a while and I came back. We were living in Hartford at the time. I met him in Hartford. [He went to the] University of Hartford. He was there as a piano performance major of all things and decided that although he was really great at the piano, he didn't have the personality to be a performance major. He's an introvert. He changed his major to biology. He ended up eventually getting a PhD in microbiology, a strange turn of events. I toured and kept coming back to him. Hartford's in a very good place because you're an hour and a half from Boston, and an hour and a half from New York. You're very well positioned to be a musician. Hartford's a good place too, and you're an hour from New Haven. We did things [at] Yale. We did things in Boston. We did things in New York. That was great, but then I wanted to have things. Living the life of a musician is great when you're twenty-three. When you're twenty-three, it's fabulous. You don't mind being poor. You don't mind living in an apartment that's 200 square feet with two other women for 1,700 a month. It's fun. You're poor. You learn things, but I wanted more. I wanted a dog, so I got married.

We moved to Nebraska. When you're a musician, you have to maintain other talents to make a living. Some years you can make a lot of money just singing. You can make a ton. Then there are other quiet months where you're not making any money. You can make $25,000 in three months, and then make nothing the rest of the year. It's just the way it goes. You can make $1,500 in a day, but then have nothing for months. So, I was a transcriptionist and a medical secretary. I transcribed for doctors. I could type fast because when you're a musician, you have piano skills. You're good with languages and you can hear things. I worked for a group of doctors in Hartford, and thankfully they were opera buffs. They would let me leave for two weeks to sing a concert. They let me leave for a month to go do a production and then let me come back. They were pretty great about that. You always retain those skills.

Then we moved here, and I found a job working as a transcriptionist for a group of surgeons in Grand Island. I worked from home, because I had to be with the babies. So, I would transcribe their letters and I emailed them up to them. That worked great. Then my kids started school and I was home. My husband and I were reading the *Omaha World Herald* one day, and we saw this thing about this nursing shortage. I was like, "I could do that." I'm not singing here. I know all the words and I know how to spell them. I don't know anything about nursing, but I know how to do a history and physical. I know how it goes. I've never touched a human. Then I realized that Creighton University had a satellite campus seven blocks away at Mary Lanning. Then Creighton had this deal where if you have an undergraduate degree in anything, you could get a nursing degree in twelve months. So, I was like, "I could do that." Of course, I didn't have any of the prerequisites. So, for sixty bucks a credit I went over to CCC and I took organic chemistry, anatomy, and physiology. I took a bunch of sciences in a year. I got a part time job as a nurse's aide at Mary Lanning just to see what nurses do before I was going to get thrown in for $42,000 at Creighton. I was like, "I really like this. I could do this." Then I learned that Mary Lanning had a scholarship. If you promise to work for them for three years, you could get that paid for. So, Mary Lanning gave me $42,000 to go to school. Who doesn't love being in school? Free education? Then a guaranteed job? What an awesome deal. I went to school for free, and then got a guaranteed job. I worked in the ER for six years, paid them back [that way]. Talk about resources. Know your value.

[In my spare time,] I love to bake bread. Before my kids left for college, I was a full-time choir mom, orchestra mom, running around and doing kid things. I was mom. I have two big dogs that my husband and I love to walk. You might even see us most nights walking through Hastings College campus. I love my dogs. I like to jog. I'm very slow, and I'm old. But you know, three miles with a podcast, and I'm pretty good. My husband's an ultra-marathoner. Really, I'm just a wannabe, but I just like to stay healthy. I love to cook. We have good friends. I love music, obviously.

We did martial arts together [as a family]. It was a thing that we could do together as a family, because we have such varied and different talents and things that we'd like to do. We are the parents of two young women, and we wanted our daughters to be able to defend themselves in the world. We took Taekwondo. I'll tell you, my elder daughter was bullied in the fourth grade and once she was adept at Taekwondo, nobody picked on her ever again. It took one round kick to the head. There's no need for that, but I feel better sending my kids off to college, knowing that they could hurt somebody that tries to hurt them.

My elder daughter is in the Honors Program at University of Kansas. She is studying political science and Arabic. She's going to spend her next semester in the Middle East because every mother wants to send her Jewish daughter to the Gaza Strip, so she can meet with the Palestinians and bring peace. She probably will go to law school. That's the plan for her. She thinks she wants to do immigration law. She's very socially and politically active. We hate to use the word social justice warriors. She hates that, but she's a social justice warrior.

My younger daughter is a sophomore at Grinnell, in Iowa. She is studying English literature. She's going to do a Shakespeare fellowship next year at the Newberry Library in Chicago. She's not as much social justice. She's more grace justice, but she's *that* kid. She's the valedictorian. Academically smart sometimes.

We spent so much time being off time. When you're on time, you're going to graduate at an appropriate age. You're going to get a job. You'll find a life partner. You might have kids, or you might not, but you'll probably do it all at the appropriate time. We did everything wrong and off time. When I friends were all finished with school and buying homes. Michael was still working on his PhD, and we were living in the city. When they were all having babies and driving Volvos, we were struggling and making ends meet and having a kid that we weren't really expected to have at the right time. Right. So, we didn't buy our first home until we were in our mid-thirties, and it was here. I had jobs, but they were sporadic because I was a musician. We always tried to do things that we could do as a family whenever we could. So, [we] don't really [have any] set traditions. We would go on the fly. Sometimes, I do regret that. We live in Nebraska, so we have Christmas. Why? Because it's Christmas in Nebraska. Our kids [went] to Alcott, the only place in the country where you can go into a public school and there are Christmas trees. Try that in West Hartford, Connecticut, and there'd be seventy-five lawyers. You can't do that anywhere else in the country. That's fabulous that we do it here. That's great. I'm sure if my kids walked in the school and said, "We want a menorah in the class," they would have been fine. That's okay. You can't have a menorah in class in Boston or Hartford. You can't have anything, because that's separate. But here, it's okay. So, we had Christmas. We had Hanukkah. We're both, so we celebrate. We would have gingerbread houses with menorahs in them.

My daughters were [treated badly in this town]. Little kids are ignorant. They don't know. They only know what they hear. When Macy was in the fifth grade at Longfellow. They hear the word Jew and the only time they'd ever heard those words was on *South Park*. The way the kids would spew those words, Macy was just horrified. That was when the Taekwondo came in handy. We had a conversation with the principal. The principal said, "Oh, this is totally unacceptable. We won't let this happen." It continued to happen. At which point I told Macy that she had my permission to use a side kick to kick to anybody [who was cruel to her]. She could employ her Taekwondo, and she did. Then she got in trouble, and then I supported her.

I [raised] my kids with the same values everybody raises their kids with. Be a good neighbor. Be a good person. Honesty. Do unto others. Servant leadership, true leaders are born in serving others. Those are the things you instill in your kids. You can't be a leader unless you're serving someone else. Just be nice. That's all. That's all you can do. I've struggled with that with my younger daughter. I think sometimes when she wasn't, she would get that back at her. I'd say, "Grace, why are you upset?"

"They were mean to me."

"Well, what did you do?" I was never one of those parents that ran to the school and said, "My daughter has been treated unfairly."

I call [Hastings] "Leave it to Beaver" land. I call it a throwback. We've lived here [for] sixteen years, and I don't even know where the keys to my house are. I have never locked my house. My kids would walk to Alcott, and I'd get a call from my neighbor, Denny. He'd say, "Julie, I saw your kids walking home from school. It's 20°F out, and Macy wasn't wearing her hat." Where else in the world do people care about your kids? I know that if my kids went to the movies on a Saturday and if they misbehaved, they'd be in trouble before they ever got home. I would know because somebody knows your kids. People care about each other around here. If somebody has a family tragedy, the next thing you know there's a pancake feed. Nowhere else in the country does this happen. People care about each other. That's what I tell people about Hastings.

I love living here. I've noticed young adults will graduate high school, and the first thing they do they can't wait to get out of here. When it comes time to settle down and raise a family, they're back. If I were young and single, I don't think I'd want to be here. If I were young and married and raising a family, what a great place to be. I love the people in town. They're compassionate. They're kind for the most part. Politically I am not on the same page as most of the state, so that's kind of a challenge for me.

Folks don't realize you can drive through six New England states in the amount of time it takes to get from here to Omaha. I was living in Connecticut, but you can get from Connecticut to Rhode Island, to Massachusetts, to New Hampshire [in] three hours. The cost of living is low. There's no traffic. [But] there are things I don't love about Nebraska. I miss the trees. I miss the ocean. I miss the mountains. I miss the trees the most.

It's a small town. I think the thing about a small town is just gossip. You hear about people very quickly. The word spreads. I don't care about that sort of thing, but even my neighbors are like, "Oh, did you hear about so-and-so?"

The college is a very vibrant part of the community. I like when they have concerts and lectures. I wish they would advertise those things better to let people know that stuff is going on. But, that's not the college's job. I think we do a great job for a little community. Our downtown has been revitalized, with our little microbreweries and restaurants. I like that there are small businesses that are doing well. We have a very active YMCA. I think that's one of the best things in our town.

Nebraskans are so much warmer. They're just nicer people. When we first moved into our house, within the first twenty-four hours, people had come over with a banana bread, a batch of cookies, or a hot dish. I didn't know what that was when I moved here. Here, people would come over and welcome you and want to know what church you go to. I have never felt unwelcome here. I really do love living here. I love meeting people. That's part of nursing too. It's caring for people and meeting people and meeting their families and nurturing.

adolfo diaz-vargas

Interviewed by Walker Hermann

I was born in Mexico. I came here when I was three years old. I'm currently working at Dramco Tool in Grand Island. [I was born in] a small state in Mexico called Aguascalientes. I have a stepdad. I don't really know my real dad. I came to the United States with my mother. She's from the same place that I was born. My stepdad is from Mexico [too]. [We moved to the US] to give myself, and the rest of my siblings, a better life. There's six of us and my mom was a single mother in Mexico. She would work three jobs [and] was basically out working all the time. It's really popular, obviously, for parents to come to the United States. She actually came here before bringing us. She was here for two years and my sister took care of me. Then she met my stepdad here. They decided to move in together and then decided to bring us. There's nine [siblings] total. [My oldest sister] is thirty-one. [I'm] twenty. There's six guys [and] three girls.

Every night we eat dinner together, and we go to church every weekend. I'm a Roman Catholic, I guess. But really, I'm neither. [My mother] is a strong

Christian. Since we were little, we were into the Roman Catholic stuff. Then my sister converted into open Christianity, and [my mother] followed in her footsteps. I'm not really into religion. Ever since high school I stopped going to church. They still currently take the younger ones to church somewhere in Grand Island. We used to go to Saint Cecilia. Other activities we do frequently? We usually just get together a lot for any little thing. We get together, maybe make some food, share some time together. [We] sit down [at the] same table and take the time to talk.

For me, Spanish was the language at home, but it was easy for me to pick up English. I wouldn't know cultures here versus in Mexico. I've lived a double life my entire life, speaking Spanish [at] home. My mother doesn't really speak English. My dad does, though. Basically, from home to school was way different. It was kind of like a two-life thing.

I've gone to Hastings Public Schools my whole life. I went to preschool here, and then kindergarten. I went to preschool at Head Start, and then I went to Morton Elementary kindergarten through fifth grade. For sixth to eighth [grade I went to] Hastings Middle School, then Hastings High. I went to Central Community College and got my drafting and design technology degree. I'm actually moving to Lincoln to go to SCC and get my engineering degree.

I worked [at Sanchez Plaza] the summer [after] eighth grade and basically until this year, actually. I just quit about two months ago. My sister ended up marrying the owner. So, it kind of turned into a family business. My older brother started working there before me. He was a manager there. My sister also works there. Basically, everyone in my family does. My mom currently works there every once in a while to help out.

I'm able to work and live in the United States under DACA status. DACA stands for Deferred Action for Childhood Arrivals. You have to meet a lot of requirements. You have to have entered the United States by a certain date. I don't know what date, but let's say if you got here the day after that day, you're not eligible for it. You had to be under [a] certain age when you came into the United States, and even currently. Let's say the cap is at thirty years, and you turn thirty two days before that date, then you're too late. It allows me to get a social security number and be able to work here. It prevents me from getting deported. So, let's say for some reason I get pulled over and then immigration gets a hold of me. I can't get deported through DACA, unless [I] get into serious trouble. They do extensive background checks. You have to have zero criminal history, even a DUI would make you not qualify for it. Then, we had to provide evidence here, every month since 2001. We had to scavenge around and find everything, medical bills, anything. One thing that people think is that people on DACA receive federal benefits, like social security insurance and stuff like that. We don't. We pay taxes. We pay social security, but we don't receive it. [The] only benefit is not being able to get deported and being able to work. I think Nebraska was the last state to allow DACA people to get a driver's license.

[Hastings is] a really peaceful place. You can actually have a really good childhood. Unlike big cities, you don't have to worry about violence. You don't have to worry much about that. You have a lot of freedom here. You can go out at night and not worry about anything. [Hastings has] really nice, caring people. I mean, if someone needs help, let's say a car breaks down, really anybody will stop by and try to help you out. [The best part of Hastings] would be my family. My entire family's here. [The worst part of Hastings] is the limited activities you can do with your friends. You gotta go to different towns to do different things, even just for the mall. There's a lack of social places you can just hang out at.

I think I will live here for the rest of my life. I honestly don't think I can say I've ever felt discriminated against because I'm Mexican, or anything like that. I've never felt discomfort that I'm not white. Everybody has been so nice.

chad dumas and dawn vincent dumas

Interviewed by Veronica Schermerhorn

My name is Dawn Vincent Dumas and my husband is Chad Dumas; he's younger than I am. We've been in Hastings for seven years and moved around a bit since we've been married for employment purposes, but so far, we only stayed in Nebraska. I am employed as a hospice nurse. We have two boys. One's in college and one's a senior in high school. We like our dog and to travel.

[Dawn] The reason I knew of the faith is because, my sisters [converted to] Bahá'í in the '70s when a lot of people were exploring different things and embracing different ways of life. It worried my parents a little bit, but their Methodist minister said not to worry. It was an okay religion to join in, they're going be alright. I grew up in a home with Bahá'í, but they were older than me. They weren't living with us, so I knew about the faith, but it was one of those things that we didn't talk about. It was a source of discontent. My parents weren't very happy about it. It wasn't like they pulled away; in fact, quite the opposite, they made a concerted effort to be part of the family. I knew about the faith; we just didn't really talk about it. As I got older, I became more curious and I spent more time with them. I decided that I wanted to do some closer investigation, and then I became a Bahá'í.

I've been a Bahá'í since I was twenty and it took me awhile to determine that's what I wanted for myself. I knew that that was right for me in my life. I traveled. I lived for a while at a Bahá'í boarding school in Canada. I did volunteer work there, and everyone was either a Bahá'í themselves or was a part of the school community, was aware of the faith and it was run along Bahá'í principles. It was a wonderful experience to be there. It was right after I became Bahá'í, I thought that it sounded like a wonderful opportunity and I said "Yes, I would like to go."

[Chad] One of the most important teachings of Bahá'í faith is independent investigation for truth. This idea that we shouldn't believe other people because they said it [but instead] we should investigate for ourselves, see with our own eyes, rather than the eyes of others. Even though my parents became Bahá'í when I was young, and I was raised knowing about the Bahá'í faith. In the Bahá'í faith the age of maturity is fifteen. That's when you decide if Baha'u'llah is who he says he is. If so, then I'm going to abide by the laws that he's given us. When I was in the early years of high school, freshmen, I went to different churches in town. I was a musician, so I played the piano at one church, the bells at another church. I got to find out a lot about the different faith communities in North Platte. I investigated Islam, Judaism, Hinduism, Zoroastrianism, Buddhism, and decided that, God has sent different messengers at different times because He loves us and wants to educate us. That's basically the essence of it; it's all a part of the same revelation from God. There's only one God. All these religions are unfolding the plan of God over time. Today is the time where we can recognize that. All the previous messengers, prophets pointed to the same; there will come a time eventually, you know, the promised one and the unification of all humankind and that Baha'u'llah is that one who they were all pointing to this is that time that the unity of humankind can be established. I became a Bahá'í at fifteen.

[Dawn] Somebody once asked me is, "What was it like when I became a Bahá'í?" This person implied that I became a Bahá'í because Chad was a Bahá'í. But no, I was already a Bahá'í when I met him. We met when we were both living in Lincoln. I was finishing up my nursing program, and he just came back from the Bahá'í World Center and he was starting his program. We met at different Bahá'í gatherings in Lincoln and wasn't too long after that. We went separately and met so that's nice.

[Dawn] The way I understand our faith's teachings is that this life is to prepare us for the next life, just as the life of the baby in the womb is to prepare that baby for the life here. In the womb, the baby has no need for eyes, no need for a mouth, no need for arms, legs really. They're kept tight in there because their arms and legs are squished up, right? There's nothing to do with them except kick me. It's all preparation, right? Then they're born into this world and then there's evidence of why they need eyes, a nose, a mouth, arms, and legs. This world then is to prepare us for the next and what we need for the next world is virtues. Any virtue that you can think of: integrity, love patience, trustworthiness, and so on. We need all of them to be our spiritual arms and legs for the next world so that we can have what we need there. We won't have these arms or legs, but we will have our virtues to do whatever we do there. Our job is to acquire virtues, practice them, and live by them.

[Chad] Baha'u'llah has written a book of laws; it's called the Kitáb-i-Aqdas, the most holy book, which is kind of interesting. He says this is the most holy book. When people think of laws, they think of do this, don't do that, right? He frames this idea of laws in a completely different way than what we think of in other religions and in society. He says, observe my commandments for love of right and not out of fear. There are these laws that are here for protection of ourselves and assistance to ourselves. Some of those laws include daily prayer and daily reading from the writings. There's a period of fasting that is in March of every year. Bahá'ís around the world fast during that time. The new year is March 20th or 21st or 22nd depending on when the first day of spring falls. The nineteen days before that, there's nineteen months, nineteen days in each month. Number nineteen is important in the Bahá'í faith. That's because the word in arabic numbers and letters correspond with each other. It's very important. The word for unity is *vahid,* and that numeric value is nineteenth. There's nineteen months with nineteen days in each, which means a few days for a time of celebration that's placed before the last month. The last month is a time of fasting before the new year. He [Baha'u'llah] forbids backbiting and gossip. He says it's worse than murder. He forbids murder. He says you shouldn't have sex outside of marriage.

[Dawn] Just to clarify, the fasting is from sunrise to sunset. We get up, we have breakfast, then we fast throughout the daylight hours, no food or drinking. Then we break the fast every evening with a meal, water or tea. We're not actually not eating; we're having that discipline of restricting our bodily desires for the daylight hours.

[Chad] You've probably not heard of it [Bahá'í] because it's the newest of the world's religions. I have a friend of mine [who] says, you know, there aren't many of us, but we're everywhere. It's the second most widespread religion, right after Christianity. I don't know if you're familiar with the history of Christianity, but right around forty years or so, the Pope declared that Christianity had covered the entire face of the earth, and it still does. Bahá'í faith was founded about 150 years ago. If you're familiar with the history at about 1840, there was a lot of religious enthusiasm throughout the world for the coming of the promised one in Judaism, the Messiah, Christianity, the second coming, and Islam, the return of the twelfth Imam, in Buddhism, the fifth Buddha. So, like these religions teach about a great time when this promised one comes in the middle of the 1840s. In the US and Europe, Christian scholars calculated that it was going to happen in 1844, October 20th was the exact date. You can go back and look at history; it's known as the great disappointment. There were significant gatherings all over the US and Europe. Even in Congress, people wore ascension robes. Some people went out and committed crimes because they figured that the next day they were going to be scooped up in the rapture.

[Dawn] Yeah, people didn't harvest their crops. It's October and they didn't harvest their crops because they didn't think they were going to need them.

[Chad] There was a lot of expectation, but just as Christ said, you know, coming as a thief in the night, he doesn't come knock on your door and say, "Hey, I'm here." They come in, they sneak in, and they sneak out, and you don't even know that they'd been there except that you see remnants of something's happened. Right? That's what happened. In the Middle East, a gentleman whose title is the Bab, it's Arabic, it means the gate. He said, and again in the 1840s he said, the promised one is near, and you need to get ready for it. He said it's close and I'm the gate through which this promised one is going to come. That's where his name, the Bab, came from. The religious leaders in Iran didn't like that. Even though he had tens of thousands of followers within a very short time [of] his ministry, which lasted six years, they killed him. One of his followers was a man whose title is the Baha'u'llah, which is again Arabic, and it means the glory of God. That's where the name Bahá'í comes from, Baha. The "i" means follower. Follower of Bahá'í. So, Baha'u'llah a follower of glory, the glory or light. Baha'u'llah was born very wealthy to a family. Even though the Persian government killed so many of these Bab'is, they couldn't kill Baha'u'llah because he was in this important position. They threw them in the worst prison they could find. Hoping he would die because they normally did, but he didn't. Then they decided to exile him, and he was exiled from place to place.

Everywhere he went, people would flock to him and loved him and loved his teachings which were there is only one god. It doesn't matter if you call him Allah or God or Yahweh or Jehovah or table cloth. It's the same, right? The sun is the sun and it doesn't matter what you call the sun. It's always producing heat. He said that you know that this god, like the sun, sends messengers because we can't look at the sun directly. Otherwise we burn our eyes, right? God sends us these mirrors, perfect to reflect his light, and so we can look in those mirrors and see how that's God. Right? And you see these messages saying, I am God and that's true. He's unknowable, but He sends these messengers to us to educate us and then there's of course the spirit that flows through them. Then you know, the rays of light and so and then now is the time for us to be able to recognize that and to come together as unity, and so the most important teaching of the Bahá'í faith is unity. Baha'u'llah was exiled throughout to the, you know, Acre [in present-day Isreal]. He died there in 1892, and then since he established a covenant with his followers, for the first time [in] the religious history, you didn't have a break off.

When you have Islam broke off into Shia and Sunni right away, and Christianity you had the Eastern Orthodox [and the] Catholics. All these spaces have division. And Baha'u'llah said, you know, after him look to his oldest son, Abdul Baha. Abdul Baha visited the US in 1912 and traveled across the US by train, stopped in Lincoln. He was pen pals I guess with William Jennings Bryan, and William Jennings Bryan, when he was in Israel, stopped to visit Abdul Baha, but he wasn't there unfortunately. Then after a while when he was here, he stopped to visit Bryan. Unfortunately, he wasn't there either, so they, like, left notes for each other back and forth. Abdul means servant. Abdul Baha, servant of glory. After Abdul Baha, he appointed his oldest grandson; he'll be authentic, and now today we have an elected body that's called the Universal House of Justice, and they guide the work around the world. There's this administrative system to keep the Bahá'í faith alive and to promote the teachings. The Universal House of Justice is the supreme governing body of the world. That's where they meet in that building. So that's the seat, the Universal House of Justice. They are elected. They're completely democratically elected in a unique system that doesn't exist anywhere. In the Bahá'í electoral process, any adult, twenty-one years of age or older, who's a Bahá'í votes in this process. It starts at the local level. Bahá'ís around this country will get together to elect a delegate to go to the national level and then elect the national assembly. When we come together, there is no electioneering, no campaigning, no nominations, no parties, no anything, any Bahá'í in good standing is eligible to be elected as the delegate. In a prayerful atmosphere, we pray, and on a sheet of paper on the ballot, we write the name of one person who we think best combines the qualities. So best combines the necessary qualities of selfless devotion, unquestioned loyalty, recognizability and mature experience. Each person prays and says, okay, who's that person for this unit? Who best combines those qualities? They write down the name of that person, secret ballot, then they're tallied and whoever has the most votes becomes a delegate. And it's as simple as that. And then it goes to the national level. And those delegates, 171 delegates from around the US, gather in at the national center, which is north of Chicago, and each year elect the national assembly and that's done in the same manner. Prayerful, no campaigning, no electionary, no nominations, nothing like that. And then in that case, then you write down the names of nine individuals. And then the nine highest vote[s] get to become the national assembly. And there's about 200 national assemblies. They gathere at Haifa, Israel, and they elect the Universal House of Justice, every five years. And then every local community that has at least nine Bahá'ís will elect a local spiritual assembly. Aurora, Lincoln, Omaha, Bellevue. They all have spiritual assemblies.

[Dawn] Hastings itself has three adult Bahá'ís and one youth; you just saw him walk through the door. We just don't have the numbers to support a Bahá'í center yet. It's a small community right now as we grow, maybe someday that will be referred to as a Bahá'í center, but there isn't right now. Right now, we gather in each other's homes and say prayers together and socialize together. And if there's any business that needs to be taken care of, let's do that as well. And um, you know, make plans like for example, almost a year ago, it was the 200th anniversary of the birth of the Bab, so that was a big celebration that we held, and we hosted a large lunch at the YWCA, and we had a video that we showed about about his life and the dramatic death. So that was, you know, a community event that was planned for by all of us. And then there's, you know, there are Bahá'ís everywhere. There are Bahá'ís in Grand Island or Bahá'ís in Aurora. There are Bahá'ís in Kearney. Even the little bitty town west of here called Curtis has Bahá'ís there. But say in Raleigh, North Carolina, it would, you'd be hard pressed to find someone who doesn't know that there are Bahá'ís in North Carolina and also South Carolina. There are many Bahá'ís. In fact, if you were to do a Google search of, you know, I don't remember how it's termed, what's the second most common religion in South Carolina? And the first of course is Christianity if you include all the denominations, including

Catholicism. The second is the Bahá'í faith. There are places even in the United States where the faith is very common, very common.

[Chad] One of the unique aspects of the Bahá'í faith is that Baha'u'llah, as he was a prisoner for all these years, for forty years, he was in exile as a prisoner. His fellow prisoners would write down revelation[s] as he spoke, and he himself would write down as well. We have in his own handwriting and then translated into English, um, prayers and writings, over 100 volumes of these. One of the teachings of the of Baha'u'llah is that each person is responsible for their own spiritual development. We can't place that on a priest or pastor or rabbi. It's on each of us. Each day we pray every morning, every evening, he said, everyday bring yourself to account and pray every morning, every evening read from the holy writings. There're these beautiful prayers that then we can pray every day.

[Dawn] So we have prayer books because, you know, as Chad was saying that at the age of fifteen people will make their own decision. We probably have a prayer book here that was Chad's when he turned fifteen. When I became a Bahá'í, you know, I was given a prayer book and suddenly that as years go on, prayer books become, we accumulate many. So here we have a few of the prayer books and then of course our children have their own prayer books. And so here we have prayer books, lots of prayer books. This one was given to me by my dear, dear friend back in 1990, so I'm not giving that one away. Chad has one from his, you know, when he was a kid and you know, when I became Bahá'í, and when we became parents, we got the Bahá'í prayers for women and spiritual strength for men.

[Chad] So the prayers are not organized. I mean they're, they're organized by somebody for the sake of ease of identification. But like Baha'u'llah, didn't sit down and say, okay, here's the age assistance prayers, here's the prayers for the departed, prayers for spiritual qualities. Somebody kind of put them in order. There are prayers from Baha'u'llah, prayers from the Bab. And then also prayers from Abdul Baha who was, uh, Baha'u'llah's son. Many of the prayers are in all the books, but then some of them have unique ones like the one for women. And because there's so many writings of Baha'u'llah, they're still being translated. So there's new prayers that are being translated all the time. It's such a blessing because no, I don't have, you know, I can come up with my own prayers. Right, right. But there's also these beautiful prayers that are just, they touch my heart. They say what I want to say anyway without having to struggle with the words.

[Dawn] I thought maybe I would find it, a prayer here for tests if I can find the one I'm thinking of. When I was in college, I would say it on my way out the door before I would go take a big test, which I don't know whether that's a good idea or not, but I did it. "I had drew Thee by Thee might. Oh my God, let no harm beset me in times of tests. In moments of heedlessness, guide my steps aright through Thine inspiration. Thou art God. Potent art Thou to do what Thou desires. No one can withstand Thy will or thwart Thy purpose." The Bab.

[Chad] "Oh, God. Refresh and lighten my spirit. Purify my heart, illumine my powers. I lay all my affairs in thy hand. You are my guide and my refuge. I will no longer be sorrowful and greedy. I will be a happy, joyful human. Oh, God, I will no longer be full of anxiety. Nor will I let trouble harass me. I will not dwell on the unpleasant things of life, oh God, Thou art more friend to me than I am to myself and I dedicate myself to Thee."

[Dawn] So in our faith, we don't have anything to signal the end of the prayer. We don't say amen. Right. Sometimes the prayers have a rhythm that you can hear, and you know when the prayer is over.

[Dawn] I am a hospice nurse. Thankfully I believe in the next world, which I think if I wasn't sure about that with certainty, it would be harder, to be honest. I don't, you know, I'm just speculating because I do not believe that certainty that there is a next world, and that part of what I do is as a nurse I have the clinical obligations of making sure they're comfortable. But I also try hard to help a person be peaceful as well. I can't assume that they believe in the next world, but maybe they can have a sense of calm and peace. So, that stuff is very much a part of my work.

[Chad] I'm the director of learning for Hastings Public Schools, and the way that I translate my faith into work is Baha'u'llah says, and I love this, he says, "Work, when it's performed in a spirit of service, is worship." So, I try to remember when I'm going to work, I'm really going to service. So that sort of refrains in my work. Our oldest son DL just got back in June. He did a year of service at the World Centre for the Bahá'í faith in Haifa, Israel as well, and whenever we would talk to him on the phone, he would refer to going to service. He never talked about going to work. The whole time he was there. And it struck us, and so I try to remember now I'm not going to work, I'm going to service because that just reorients it, and then then it's like worship. You know, every job has its challenges. I would say this one has its challenges too, but there are more better days than worse days.

[Chad] I don't think I have [been discriminated against] in Hastings. I know I have. I didn't get a job once because of it. In Lincoln, they had a change in pastors. I'd been the choir director for two and a half, three years and they had a change. Everybody knew I was Bahá'í, but then they had a change in pastors, she didn't like that. So, I resigned. They didn't release me.

[Dawn] They would have, they would have. But you didn't let it go that far. I don't worry about it. It doesn't bother me. I think that it would be good if we could have a conversation, you know, if we can talk and, I can help them to understand where I'm coming from if possible. Sometimes it's not possible. Um, and it's okay. You know, it's okay. Everybody, in my opinion, everyone is doing the best they can. They're trying to live their best life. They have the best interests of themselves and their community at heart for the most part. Now there are a few exceptions, but those are very rare, and I don't usually hang out with them anyway, so I'm not likely to run into somebody who doesn't have their best interest of the community. I don't worry about it. That's fine.

[Chad] Well, I remember when I, I'm thinking of a job, the job I didn't get, which was also a church to be acquired for a director position because that's what my bachelor's degree was in. I remember feeling really happy that I had this opportunity to sacrifice in my way for my faith and also felt relieved and blessed that that now I wouldn't have to work in an environment that would have been hostile towards me anyway.

[Dawn] Our son tonight is showing a video to the UNK Social Justice League about the persecution of the Baháʾís in Iran. You asked us about persecution and discrimination. We do not have what they have, right? What they have is unemployment because no one will hire them at all. They start their own businesses, and then the government comes and chained the doors closed so they can't have no business even. Then what they do is they bring their business out on the sidewalk in front of the business so that they can make a living. What are you supposed to do? Right? They get in this film that he's showing, the young people that are trying to go to college, get kicked out. Because in Iran, you have to say what religion you are. Right? And if you're not Muslim, what are you? Well, I'm a Baháʾí. So then out, no college for you. There's a video that he showed tonight at UNK. It's called *Education Is Not a Problem*.

[Chad] Baha'u'llah says a wonderful quote. He says, "Be regarded as a mind rich in gems of inestimable value." Gems of inestimable, you can't even estimate the value. And then he says, "Education alone can uncover those gems." We're like this mind full of gems and ... the only way you can uncover those gems is through education. It's very, very important. Which also reminds me of, you know, the teachings of Baha'u'llah in terms of the unity of humankind, the equality of women and men. This is what made me think of it. Education is important, and the equality of women and men are so important that Baha'u'llah says that if you only have enough money to educate one of your children, the girl must take precedence. That it's that important. Educate her because she's the first educator of the next generation. So, what the Baháʼís did then is they started their own university, what's called the Baháʼí Institute of Higher Education. This persecution of the Baháʼís really ramped up after the revolution of Iran in 1979. They started an underground university where, you know, Baháʼís are well educated because education is so important. Since I'm a teacher, if I were in Iran, I would teach education classes to people who want to be teachers. We do correspondence courses and mail things back and forth and maybe meet in Grand Island one weekend. Young people would come together, and we studied together for the weekend and give assignments and you'd go out. They had this whole network of the Baháʼí Institute of Higher Education that then the governments started to shut down and arrest anybody who is participating in that. Imprison and death sentences against them. That's what this video is about, and it's a whole hashtag—#EducationIsNotaCrime. The UN and the US governments have all condemned these violations of human rights, but Iran keeps doing it.

[Dawn] In the video they show that there are mural artists who have, throughout New York City and other places, have put murals up with the hashtag, #EducationIsNotaCrime. You know, and it'll show all kinds of different things, you know, people reading stacks of books, um, someone holding bars of a prison cell. I mean there are all kinds of murals across the New York City.

[Dawn] Unfortunately, there can also be misinformation that gets spread in person. If you were to look, you can find the misinformation and it would be hard to tell the difference unless you talk to a Bahá'í who then our job is to tell you the truth. Now you, it would be your choice whether to believe the misinformation or believe in the person who's talking to you. It's hard to tell sometimes because sometimes something might sound plausible, but it's misinformed.

My name is Delta Fajardo-Norton, originally Delta Fajardo. I'm thirty-eight years old. I was born in Japan in 1979 at Yokota Air Base and lived there until I was five. [I] moved to the Philippines at Clark Air Base and lived there until I was eight and came to the United States at Bellevue in 1988. My parents were in the military, so they both worked at military bases. I am part Filipino, and part Iowan.

In Japan and the Philippines, that was all military bases. [I] went to military base schools. I remember Japan, but the Philippines had a bigger impact on me. We had a house servant, named Salia, and she was from the barrios. What happens a lot of times, these people didn't have a way to get an education. So, my dad, who's a Filipino, went to the barrios and requested her. She was able to stay at our house. She took care of everything, all the cleaning, nannying, and we helped put her through school.

In Japan, I started kindergarten when I was four, but they held me back. I did kindergarten again when I was in the Philippines. [I] did third grade all the way

delta fajardo-norton

Interviewed by Collin Fowler

through high school and college in the US. I went to Bellevue Public Schools; that's Mission Middle School in Bellevue East. Then I went to Peru State College, graduated there in 2003. [Then I] got my master's degree through UNK in curriculum and instruction in 2007. My undergraduate was language arts education, and now I have extra hours in communication so that I can teach college credit Communication Arts. I like to do theater. I haven't done it lately, but I enjoy acting. Debate is life. I [like] photography. I take photos. I do portraits. I also do artistic photography. I like to write and travel.

In the Philippines, the base was not really accepted. We were there around the time the protests were going on, and sometimes they would close off the base. We learned duck drills, where if somebody were shooting at us, we would know where to duck or how to duck.

That was an interesting time period. I think the only thing that kept my family safe was that my dad was Filipino. He paid the police off. I'm not joking. He really did pay the police to watch over us. Both my parents worked. I feel like I should have gotten kidnapped as a child because I went everywhere in the Philippines without any kind of supervision. But again, the police were there. They knew my dad.

My dad is a Fajardo. My grandfather, Tirso Fajardo, went to West Point and eventually became the commander of the Filipino army and

Commandant of the Philippines Academy. So he's well known. They have a bust of him there. There's a section of town that's named Fajardo after my great-grandfather Daniel Fajardo. So, we're really well known. That was why I was allowed to get away with the things I got away with.

[My religious background is] hardcore Catholic. My dad's area of the Philippines is very Catholic based. [We] went to church every Sunday, very strict. I know all the prayers. There was a time period where I questioned and wanted to go into a different religion, but it was so ingrained in me and so comfortable to me that I stayed Catholic. Do I have the same religious views necessarily? Not exactly, but it's comforting to me.

As a debate coach, I've told everybody that I'm never going to tell what my political views are. It's my job to have you guys see the different sides of an argument, so I don't get heavy into different politics. For this one time, I will give you a sense of my political views. To the general public, I've never actually had a side. I've given both sides. Politically, I'm registered as a Republican. Do I have a lot of the views? Not necessarily. For example, I believe in abortion. I think that's because of my background in the Philippines. You had kids who were running around the streets selling candy in high traffic and gas areas. You had kids getting sold into prostitution. It was so extreme that I wouldn't want anybody to live that way. My experiences make me both [conservative and liberal], but I'm registered Republican. I also am a hardcore believer in working hard. I think that's a Republican concept, where you work for your money, you don't get things given to you. Again, that's how I grew up and how we had a solid upbringing. They didn't just give the poor in the Philippines anything. You found a way to make money. You did whatever you could. They didn't have a whole lot of handout programs. That's how I grew up, thinking of it that way.

I loved Japan. I always thought of Japan as my home. It was so cool, so many different things, lots of technology. Both [of] my parents were military. They ended up moving to the Philippines because that was their next assignment. Then we moved to the Philippines and it was [an] island [of] palm trees and shacks. That was the thing that I remember the most, that so many people lived in shacks and you would have a brand new building here [and] a bunch of shacks all around it. It was just new and old all at once, rich and poor altogether. We left the Philippines because my mom had an assignment at Sac Air Base in Bellevue. My dad retired. I ended up growing up in Bellevue for the rest of forever. [When] I came to the US, that was a whole other life, a whole different story.

[When I went to the US, I] wasn't really prepared. I originally thought Nebraska was an island, because Japan and the Philippines were islands. My parents really didn't explain that to me. They also did not explain to me the difference in culture [between] Japan, the Philippines, [and] the military. We have all different kinds of culture around us. Bellevue is predominantly white. That was an eye-opening experience, and I'm white.

Before my parents got a house here, I stayed with my grandmother in Rock Rapids, Iowa until they found a house. We had to sell her house. So, we had to live in this apartment area for a couple weeks, before we were able to actually transfer out of the base that they call housing. We were stuck in an apartment. Imagine five people living in military apartments.

I have four siblings; Deborah, Donna, David, Daniel. We all came with my mom and my dad. We [had to] leave behind our dog, Jazz. We [also] left Salia. I loved Salia. She was like a second mom to me. I did not understand why she had to stay behind, why she couldn't pick up, move to our country, and continue having a job there. We [left] my dad's side of the family who is still there, the Fajardo side of the family. Interestingly, I know this is going to sound weird, but I left behind my confidence in the world. When I moved here, I was suddenly an outcast, and I didn't understand why.

I was forced to come here. When I had an opportunity to leave, because I always wanted to go back to Japan because I saw it as home, I actually kind of grew in love with Hastings, the people, the culture. It's quiet. I feel like I can bring up a family here. I think about bringing up a family in Japan or the Philippines and even in [the] Bellevue area. I feel like here, it's safe. I can always travel to all these other other places and give them that culture.

In Hastings, there's more acceptance. Whenever I was on base, I was accepted because they had a lot of different cultures there. Everybody understood moving in and moving out. That is the biggest similarity [between here and my old homes]. The biggest difference was milk. Milk tasted so bad. When I moved to the US, I had to drink milk with Captain Crunch because it was so sweet. I had to use Captain Crunch to get used to it. For four months, I couldn't drink milk from the US. My sister-in-law, who is Filipino, came over and she said the exact same thing. So, I know it wasn't me.

In the Philippines, we were really accepted. We were the popular ones, the go-getters, the confident ones. I was hoping it was going to be the exact same here. Initially, it wasn't. After having [my mentor] in my life and becoming a teacher, definitely. A big hope was that I would continue to travel and experience things. I travel a lot. I even take random trips. I'm serious. I go to the Eppley Airfield, and I'm like, "Huh, where do I want to go? Hey, Asheville looks good." So, I get on my computer. That night, I'm going to Asheville. I try to do that once a year.

When I came to the United States, I didn't understand that biracial marriages were not acceptable. Immediately, I was an outcast. I was called a mutt because [of] cross-breeding. I was called a faker. I was called white chocolate, those kinds of things. Then we had a group of boys who [each] made it their life's mission to make me miserable. [For] example, I used to play the clarinet, and when I had my first concert, these boys literally sat in front of me on purpose and pointed at me the whole time. I squeaked twice, and then I never picked up the clarinet again. They tried to drown me in a pool. I know they tried to drown me in a pool because at that time in my life, I was able to swim the length of an Olympic pool without breathing. I was down there for a long time. They pounded their feet on my back, and I had bruises. So, I played like I was dead. Why didn't the lifeguard stop them? They were in on it. They didn't care. I was not normal. They wrecked my bicycle at the pool, and lifeguards didn't stop them. Nobody saw anything.

Later on, the same boys tried to become my friends. Supposedly, they came over to my house one time, and they were like, "We were bad, but we want to be friends now. Why don't you come out and play?" They were the popular kids. So I was like, "Okay, great. Yes. Finally, I'm not going to be an outcast anymore." I go out the front door, [and] I walk down the street. [Then] they come out from these bushes, and they're throwing tomatoes at me. By my seventh grade year, those people who were my friends kicked me off the lunchroom table. I sat in a social studies room for two years and ate lunch alone. It wasn't until I got into high school that things changed.

I went from a place where I was completely accepted for being different, to a place that was totally unaccepting of my differences. It took my seventh grade teacher, Mrs. Wilkinson. She's my forever mentor. She told me I was going to do a speech for 4-H. I was scared, but I trusted her. I did well. I got district and went to state and eventually, I felt strong enough to join the choir. In college, I did show choir. That's why I say I left my confidence back in the Philippines. It was beat out of me when I came here. I feel like I'm respected [now]. I feel like my differences actually make people want to know more about me. As a teacher, I feel like a lot of the students like me. I feel like people take me seriously and try to get help. I'm a helper. I help people.

My first impression, on the fun side, [was that] I thought [Nebraska] was an island and I [would be] surrounded by oceans. Then I came here. It was oceans of corn. It's very flat and very cold. I was used to eating with chopsticks and spoons. My grandmother, on my mom's side, wacked me over the head and told me I needed to use my fork when I was eating peas. I tried to use the fork and the peas kept falling off. Finally, I just got so frustrated. So, I used the fork to scoop the peas into the spoon. I ate with a spoon. She gave up on me.

Then there's the other side of it, the feeling of an outcast. It changed because of Mrs. Wilkinson. I got really confident and I became a teacher because I wanted to make a difference. I wanted to be just like her. Now I teach debate. This is my sixteenth year teaching English, nine teaching Communications. I tell [my students] this exact story the first couple of days in my class, because they're so scared of giving speeches for Communication Arts. I tell them this whole story and I tell them, "I should not be here. I should have never become a teacher. I shouldn't be in front of you giving this speech right now." Because, statistically speaking, somebody who grows up as an outcast and is bullied the way I was bullied is supposed to hate school, not do well in school, not go to college, intend to just have a low-end paying job. I go against the norm, and it took one person to change that. Now, I live to try and show people that difference. I live to give them a voice, and I live to be silly, because I lived in a shadow for a good portion of my life. And now I don't care; I'm going to enjoy it.

I am married to Michael Norton. We've been married for seven years. It was my first year teaching, and I didn't know anything about debate, especially Congress. He was a senior, and he knew everything about Congress. He had to teach me. Now, we didn't actually meet or date until 2008. I was in a serious relationship. He was in his own high school relationship. In fact, I hated him because he would always come to class late. Then he graduated, left for a couple years, came back, [and] asked if he could be an assistant coach. From there, he kept asking me if I would date him. I was like, "No, duh." Interestingly, teachers, friends of mine, and even the principal at the time were very accepting. My teacher friends were like, "You guys are perfect. Why not?" In 2008, he asked me to marry him and we got married in 2011. That was awkward.

Michael owns Video Kingdom now. I help out with that. Sometimes he helps out with debate because he's good at that. We both like to go travel. We both enjoy watching anime; Japanese grew up with that. [We do] a lot of movie watching and sleeping because we're both really tired from our jobs. We hang out with friends, [and] we do the Elks club.

[Some traditions we try to establish are] taking our shoes off at the front door. That's definitely an Asian and Filipino thing. We try to alternate on holidays. One year, we do Thanksgiving with my family, another year with him, same with Christmas. To be honest, we haven't been able to really create a whole lot of traditions because we just move. We had a house out in Westbrook for six years, but we were so busy that we never actually made it a home. We didn't even take things out of boxes. We didn't have pictures on our walls, because we were just that busy. Now that we have this new home, we're really going to make it a home.

Here with Hastings, I don't like that it is small. For example, I was very concerned when I did finally make the decision to date my husband. I did not feel comfortable going on dates in Hastings because everybody knew everybody. We ended up having to try and have a courtship outside [of Hastings]. We'd go to Grand Island, Lincoln, [and] Omaha. We were really forced to keep it quiet. There was this fear that [the people of Hastings] wouldn't be accepting. That sounds ridiculous, paradoxical, but it is the case. A lot of it has to do with being a teacher, first of all, and then my childhood of people not being very accepting.

[Hastings needs to] continue to grow in terms of diversity. Just as an example, I went to Norfolk and they have an Indian restaurant. It was a week old and they were like, "Wow, that's completely unexpected." I love Ninja here. I would love it if they had an Indian restaurant here. I would love it if they had a Filipino restaurant here. We have the population to do that kind of stuff. We have a huge Vietnamese population. Why don't we have a Vietnamese restaurant? They have one in Grand Island. The more they seem to be focusing on revitalizing downtown, the more they are opening up to a lot of different cultural things. If there were any other ways that they can improve, it would be more money towards schools so that we can better support our students.

[Hastings is] peaceful, comfortable. In some ways, it can be considered limiting, because you don't have a lot of the things that you can do in bigger cities. I feel like Hastings is really trying to change that. For example, we have a sushi place now. I go there all the time. It's very accepting. I was concerned coming here because my last name was Fajardo at the time, but I look white. I was actually scared. I was moving into a place [where] it was gonna be my childhood all over again. But no, they just welcomed it. In fact, they relished having that diversity. [It] completely took me off guard. Hastings diocese for the Catholic Church is very different than the base's Catholic Church. They're very strict here in comparison to being very open on bases. In other countries, they're trying to have more of a missionary style to try and gain more membership, versus the rigidity that's here. Hastings High School works really, really hard to try and give the best they possibly can for students. [The people in Hastings are] very accepting. I feel safe. Although, I feel like if I say one thing, it's going to make it around the town. Everybody knows everybody in all walks of life. Everybody just gets together, and we're having a good time together. The best thing about Hastings is [that] I feel so much more accepted here than I did anywhere [else] in the United States.

I am a Nebraska girl. I was born around North Platte, kind of moved around a little bit, a lot more in my earlier years. We lived there until I was about five, then moved up to Valentine and lived there till I was about twelve in 1988. I've been here [Hastings] since 2003.

There [are] a lot of positive experiences as far as Hastings. It's peaceful as compared to maybe Grand Island. I like the schools here, and I'm comfortable here. Hastings has both a small-town comfort feel, but also is beginning to have diverse experiences available for people. So, there's a lot of opportunities here. There are some of those small-town negatives; maybe too many people know your business or judge you, but I haven't experienced judgement a lot myself.

I have a Christian background. I didn't grow up in a traditional denominational, faith tradition. I grew up in a non-denominational faith tradition and so it was pretty fundamental and very conservative. I was taught some pretty hard line beliefs about, say, sexuality and so on, which were difficult. But also, I very

Interviewed by Basil Rabayda

lanae hall

much felt love from people as well. And I love God too. I felt the call into ministry, so I actually spent three years doing ministry work. It was a little bit different from your typical, pastoral experience where they go to seminary and they get ordained or whatever. I just wrote the person who is the overseer of our state, and I said, "I feel that God is calling me to be in the ministry." So, I went with somebody, and I learned from them. I didn't go to a seminary and I wasn't ordained, but I was minister for three years.

I used to be Republican for a long time because I just fell in line with what I was taught growing up. I didn't question it for a while. It seemed to be very fit and then it became clear that's not where I fit. But I didn't want to be a Democrat either because I had some problems with the division and dividing into [a] party. Some years ago, I decided to be an independent, nonpartisan.

I graduated from Alliance High School in Alliance, Nebraska. I did go to a year of college in Lincoln, and then I worked for a year and a half. That's when I went into ministry, then I got married and had kids. I decided this was part of me becoming a whole person. So, I returned to college. At that time, I went to CCC. Then I transferred to Bellevue to get my undergraduate degree in psychology. Right now, I'm almost done with my master's for counseling.

What I like about that word *queer*, is that it is very expansive. It accommodates the fluidity that I feel at present in my sexuality as well as in my gender identification. Queer is a word that's very, very malleable still. The word gay maybe [is] not as malleable anymore. It's become more set in rows. It also used to be a pejorative, so it's taking a word that had a negative connotation and turning it back and proudly owning it. I never liked the word *lesbian*, but I came out as gay, officially and publicly, three years ago. It [was] maybe six to eight months ago that I decided *queer* is the word that fits me better, and I decided to own that.

I am a mother of four children, and they're pretty fabulous. I am a proud mother and all of that. My oldest is almost fourteen and my youngest is eight. They brought light to my life. There was a space in me that I felt needed filling, and they provided that. They brought meaning to my life. The oldest two are boys, fourteen and eleven, and the girls are ten and eight. They're just amazing. They've inspired me to be a real person because they think they need to see that so that they have the courage to do that themselves. I mean, what if one of them is gay or queer or whatnot, and I wanted them to know that that's okay. I didn't want them to grow up with the same mental restrictions or binds on them that I did.

Coming out to my kids was not even a problem. I took them to a pride event with me where we had a march. They [asked], "Why is this a big deal?" I said, "Well, this is a big deal to me and it's important to me because I'm gay too." And they're like, "Oh mom, I think that's so cool." They were all for it and they were enthusiastic. They carried the rainbow flags. They thought this is the greatest thing ever.

I've been not so much overtly discriminated against. There's sort of a luxury that goes with being a sex or gender minority. It's not written on your face, like you're black and that's the skin you wear, and people see that. I can walk by and people don't know what [my] sexual orientation is, and they don't need to. It does save you a lot of grief sometimes. But if you're with a group and you are taking action, that marks you as part of the group. There have been a few times where we've experienced that with the pride march. We experienced people honk at us or flip us off. But what I chose to focus on was how much support there was in comparison to the negative displays that there were. There is hostility, but I personally have not experienced it directed toward me in any way that has harmed me greatly. I know that there's some disapproval there, but there's often a difference between disapproval and hostile actions. Some people don't understand, but they're not going to mistreat you either. I think we need more explicit safe spaces. An LGBT type of place that's for them to go and also some clear markings. Also, maybe some more events and more institutions in town doing more to show their support.

[I was born in] St. Joseph Missouri [on] April 1st, 1996. [I grew up there] on and off, here and there. I didn't have a good childhood with my mom. She mostly favored my brothers. It's just one of those things. It's just like, "What can you do?" I ended up going into foster care. Then my aunt came and got me, so I lived with her for two [or] three years. Then I moved in with my grandma because my brothers were there. Then my grandma left her husband and we moved up here when I was in second or third grade. I already lived up here with my aunt, so I just moved back. After that, it's just been a roller coaster.

My family's originally from Missouri. My great-grandma and grandpa owned a farm. They had [a] number of kids, too many to count. They all grew up there and lived in Missouri. They moved to St. Joe and then they all kind of spread ways. We're in Hastings because my uncle got a job here at the refinery, a GPA refinery. My great-grandma and grandpa followed him up here. Then everybody started just migrating this way.

Interviewed by Bailly Ballard

xyeria hayes

I went to church as a kid. I went to PULSE as a kid, but my grandma, it never really was her thing. By the time I was in third grade, I went to ten different public schools [between here and] the city of St. Joe. My mom moved that much. So, I really didn't learn, I was too focused on being acquainted with the school or knowing [that] school. It was hard ... something I'm not going to do to my kid. It's one of those things. After that I came up here and went to Longfellow. Wonderful. Wonderful. Wonderful. Anyway, I went there through fifth grade and then I went to the middle school. I went to ninth grade here for a week and then moved down to St. Joe and went to Benton High School and on to Central, but I didn't like that school. It was big, and they really favored people that play sports. Well, your bitch ain't that athletic anymore, so that one wasn't for me. I went to Benton sophomore year through senior year and graduated there. Then I start here soon at Central Community College in January. [I want to get into] early childhood education, mainly to spy on my daughter's grades, so I know what's really going on.

[In my spare time,] I hang out with my daughter. I also hang out with my aunt because she has arthritis in her hips and her knees. It's just a mess. She needs help and my grandma has dementia and she just don't remember her ass from her arm. She needs help too. I just go over there, and I deal with all the bullshit, help them and I'm just like, "Yeah, love you too."

Makeup [is my favorite hobby]. [I got into it because] it was more me doing what [I] wasn't supposed to do at [a] young age, which was going out and drinking with my friends. Sitting down and being able to do my makeup before I did that always made me feel better. [It] always really calmed my nerves or my anxiety about the night.

[I am currently] engaged. We met on Facebook. I think as a 'to be honest' status literally. Dead serious, [but] it was a deep conversation. Then it turned into us meeting through one of my really good friends, Brandi. [He, Dallas, is a] jerk. I'm just playing. He's a good guy. He works really hard for me and our daughter and provides very well. Sometimes he's a jerk, but I love him dearly. He has a good personality, a great personality. He's very caring and he's very family orientated, even with my family. My family's not the best, but he's very family orientated. He makes me be family oriented, even when I don't want to be; like, I just want to sit in the house and wallow in self-pity and like, you know, be about me. He's like, "No, you need to see your aunt and see your grandma. You need to do this now." But I'm just like, "Okay, well, let's go. Cause I'm not going alone."

I think [he's family oriented because] he didn't have that, neither one of us really. We try to give our daughter everything we didn't have, which involves us being around family constantly and making sure she sees people constantly. It's not pushing her off on people but pursuing people that actually want to see her. It's one of those things that's hard for both of us, [but] we're doing a very good job at it. It's [only hard because it's] something we don't know how to work or guide ourselves through. It's step by step, play by play. It's one of those things, and it's working out really good so far.

Let me tell you about my baby, Brealynn Lou. [I had her when] I was twenty-one. She's cute as hell, but she has a lot of me. I will never deny that. She has my attitude. I mean, she's practically all me. [We call her] Sissy. I was called Sissy as a kid by my grandma, my brothers, and so I call her Sissy. I call her Sis mostly because we tried so many nicknames that didn't stick or didn't work. Sis was just one of those things. I'm just like, "Oh my goodness, she's going to be somebody's sister one day anyway, so why not call her Sis?" It worked out. I actually got her a shirt that says, "They call me Sis," and it's white and black with glitter letters on it.

We like to go to museums [as a family]. Me and Dallas love history, and I can only hope my kid loves history as much as I do. She's really into going to museums, trust me. We won't be looking at a lot of stuff, it's more like touching, running, and climbing stairs. A lot of exercise for myself. It's less museum and more exercise, but it's a nice little gym. I get through it, all the obstacles. Christmas [is an important family tradition for us]. Oh, I've been celebrating Christmas for [the] last month; it ain't even October yet. Do I care? No. Guess why? Because it's almost Christmas.

I'm caring and outgoing. I'm very motivated to make a life for my daughter that I didn't have. I do know my talk is a little ghetto. That's just the Missouri in me. I shouldn't say that, but it just reflects where I grew up and how I was raised. My grandmother was a white, so I wasn't like raised down on Prospect Avenue in Kansas City. No, I was raised in St. Joseph, Missouri by wonderful people. My aunt is a wonderful person. Both my aunts are wonderful people. My grandma was a wonderful person. It's not that I was raised incorrectly, I was just wasn't taught about all things in life. I was taught do what you gotta do to get your money, pay your bills, go to school. My daughter means a lot to me, a whole lot. I love that little girl more than life itself.

My fiancé, on the other hand, some days he can go, but he can come right back because I love him. I love him and that he works very hard to provide for our family. He works very hard to support my dreams and life. He lets me not work so I can go to school. He lets me not work so I can do makeup. He lets me not work so I can do whatever I want to do, and he supports me in that. I couldn't ask for anybody better.

I have a very good support system. Sometimes, I'm not right in my own actions, so I look to my aunt a lot to help me with a lot of things, including raising my kid. She gets my kid four hours a day, if that, and sometimes not every day, but she goes over there. My aunt's very proper. My aunt's very clean. My aunt's very sophisticated in her way. She's very good with money. My aunt is all of that. So, if I ever have issues, I go to my aunt. My daughter goes to my aunt. At this age, if she [my daughter] gets mad at me or she has some trouble at home [she'll say], "Aunt Sue, Aunt Sue." She wants my aunt, and I have no problem with that because my aunt was such a good role model to me and still is a role model to me. She guides me through my finances half the time because I didn't learn what a credit score was or, [for example, when] you're taking out a loan, and they're going to charge you this much percent extra. I didn't learn it as a kid. The values I want to install in her [my daughter] are not ones that I was faced with, but better. I want her to know what a credit score is. I want her to know [to] put money in [her] piggy bank. She enjoys that. I'll give her $1 and she goes and gets a piggy bank and we stick the dollar in the piggy bank. Those types of things that I didn't have, she's gonna have.

She's going to be proper. She's going to be respectful. Even though I sound ghetto as hell, I'm very respectful to people. I try to be most the time anyway. I take constructive criticism, but you're not going to belittle me, because at the end of the day, I'm a person the same way you're a person. It's not okay to just talk rudely to somebody. My daughter will never do that. I mean, I hope she doesn't take those traits from me, because I can go off on somebody in like ten seconds. But, at the end of the day, I try to be very respectful.

The best thing [about Hastings, and Nebraska as a whole,] for me is the opportunity to start over again. I was here once, and I feel [that] the kind of way I live now and the way I did back then are two different things. I moved because I had to, not because I wanted to [then]. Now, everything is in my hands. It's in my ballpark. I do what I want, when I want. It's a lot nicer that I have that opportunity. Coming from where I come from, coming from St. Joe, this town is ten times cleaner [and] ten times greener. Walking downtown St. Joe was nice, but you can get mugged in frickin' two minutes. I can walk downtown here with my kid and feel perfectly safe. I do [like living here]. I honestly don't mind the people here. They probably mind me a lot more than I mind them, but, hey, what can you do?

I [do] hate how people lock their car doors [when I'm around]. I'm not going to steal their car or something. They pull their purses closer. I know I'm black, but I'm also white. I am mixed like chili. I'm not gonna mug you. I don't want your purse. I have a whole debit card with money on it. I think a lot of people think I'm a teen mom. I don't know how to describe it. I feel certain feelings when people look at my kid. But then then you have those nice people that literally stop and do nothing but talk to my daughter. I'm like, "You guys are just making her head bigger." She knows she's cute. She's [at] the point where she just smiles now. I'm just, like, "This is too many compliments [in] one day." We'll go the grocery store, go to Walmart, and everybody [is] stopping, "Oh, she's so cute, She's so cute." Oh, yeah. Yeah, she's cute. Thank you we have to go home and deal with her showing off because she thinks she's cute now. But I'll take whatever I can get.

[Hastings can become a better community] starting with that Trump flag on Seventh Street. That needs to go down. You can have your political views, but be courteous of your neighbors. Not everybody shares that political view. I'm not saying everybody has to. I'm saying how would you feel if I had a flag up in my yard that you didn't support?

Yeah, that's my right, but it's not just me in that area. You wouldn't want to see that if it wasn't something you believed in or something you didn't like. It's not just me and the community that feel that way. I just think there could be a little more thoughtfulness. There's a lot of different ethnicities here and a lot that can be offended by that. Like I said, it's their right. I feel this way, and that's fine. I just think ... treat somebody how you want to be treated.

My name is Jose Jimenez. I was born in Long Beach, California. At about three months, I moved to Mexico and that's really where I grew up. I tell people I grew up in Mexico because the first nine years of my life were in Mexico. Then [I] moved to Long Beach, California and did most of my teenage years there, until about fifteen when I moved to Lexington, Nebraska.

Lexington is where I started getting more acquainted with school. Prior to Lexington, and prior to [age] fifteen, school wasn't a priority. But at fifteen, I started to invest in myself a little bit more and then ultimately made it to Hastings for college. In Lexington I didn't know what I was doing. Long Beach to Lexington was a huge difference. So, that was a critical moment where I started to notice, "What am I doing?" The speech team recruited me there. Then the speech team for the college here in Hastings recruited me. I graduated, and now I coach the team. I am currently working for a nonprofit based out of Lincoln. We work outside of Lincoln and Omaha in the whole state, fighting for and educating people on immigrants and

Interviewed by Adam Fitzgerald

jose jimenez

the positivity that they can bring. Seeking common sense immigration laws is kind of what I'm dedicated to now. I'm dedicated to strengthening community—[that] is my cheesy explanation on my job.

My parents were originally from Mexico. They grew up there in the 1950s and 1960s. They grew up in a very different time than it is now, not as trying as it currently is. They were very excited that they met each other. They dated for about five years, in a time when my dad was from a part of the city where people weren't allowed to date people who were from my mom's side of the city. [It was] very much [a] divided community. They kept it going for five years without their parents knowing. It all accumulated to this giant destruction of the families where they said, "Whoa, what's going on?" I often like to joke that my parents are the Mexican version of Romeo and Juliet.

They lived there until the late 1980s. My grandfather applied for a visa for my dad, and my dad was able to come into the US as a resident. When he moved in, he also brought my mom and my two brothers, who were undocumented at the time. Then we went back in 1992 after I was born.

Right after I was born, my dad tried to not apply for medical benefits for me. [He] didn't want to cause a burden, [that's] how he framed it at the time. My mom decided to get WIC. WIC was the only supplement that they had. My dad at the time was working at Earl May, [a] plant nursery selling plants. Then on the side [he] would go and plant the plants that people bought from the store. He did landscaping on the side. Then around that time, the wages started dropping. Money became a problem at the time, especially with [a] newborn and two young teenagers. My brothers are ten and eleven years older than I am and [were] entering teenage years at that time. It's really difficult to have a whole family here. So, my dad sent my mom, my two brothers, and I back to Mexico. I saw my dad maybe once or twice a year because he stayed in the US working and would send us money. I knew I had a dad. I knew who he was. I knew he existed [and] was super excited when he came because he brought us toys.

It was more difficult to raise kids in the US as opposed to Mexico because the culture is very different here. I've noticed, and it's not the same. It's not universal. What I have come to notice is that, especially in my family, it was very difficult for us to find time [together]. Spatially we're very divided. You need a car to get pretty much anywhere. In Long Beach, you could get on your buses and go to your family members. In Mexico everyone walks everywhere because everything is so close. When I went back, I had the full support of all my aunts there. My mom had eight sisters. Between all of them, and my two grandmothers, I grew up among them, all of them.

We all lived very close. The whole family lived on the same street. Oftentimes the streets were named after the families that lived there. As a kid, you walked out of your house and you're hanging out with all your older cousins, younger cousins, aunts, [and] uncles. This isn't universal in our culture, but in my family [on] my mom's side, the women didn't work. That's how my mom was raised. To this day, my mom [has] only officially worked about six months of her life. That's because it was taboo in her family. My aunts were at the house always. In the US, my dad only had two brothers. One brother lived in Sacramento, which is about six, seven hours away from Long Beach. The other brother lived in Lexington, Nebraska, which was … quite a ways. My mom didn't have anybody in the US at the time. That's what made it so difficult. The family unit was not nonexistent. We survived just among the immediate nuclear family. When you're an immigrant who maybe doesn't have quite as many routes [as] some of the families who have been here for a long time, there's not enough of an infrastructure to raise a newborn.

Once my brothers found out that the legal age to work in the US was sixteen, they both said, "Hey, we're sixteen. We want to go. We want to go to the US." We [had] a wage, so we waited about a year or two

[as] my brothers were starting to save up money [and] talking about *El Norte*. We called the US, *El Norte*. There are some incredible, scary stories about *El Norte*, but overall it was clear that the chance to ride a train was possible. That alone to me, as an eight-year-old, was, like, "Holy cow, I can ride a train?! Those are real?! Didn't know that!" In Mexico, in my hometown anyway, we walked everywhere, and if you were lucky you could ride a donkey places. So, it was common for people to ride donkeys and those were your wheels at the time.

The town I grew up in is called Puruándiro, Michoâcán, which is a small community of 20,000 max. [It was] actually an indigenous community for a very long time. The tongue that was spoken there is my family's to this day. None of us speak it, but my father's grandmother still spoke that language. *Puruándiro Michoâcán* means hot springs. There is a hot spring in our city. At the time, back in the day when we didn't have indoor plumbing, we would go shower there. There were communal showers. On Mondays, the women could go in. On Tuesdays, the women with their kids could go in. Wednesday was just the men. Thursday was just teenagers, etc. Essentially, you had just one to maybe two days, if you were lucky, to shower. Everyone showered in the communal spring that sprung from the mountain. The water came from down there, and it was warm year-round.

[It is a] very small town and you've never really left your colony, it was called *colonias*. Again, because everything you did was on that street, maybe you would go down to the supermarket, which was in the central part of the city. It was a market. There were all these vendors to spread out there. Then there were some grocery stores that were just for bread, just for tortillas, or just for meat. Those existed across the city, but most people went straight to the market where you could find everything nearby. That was always the cool trip. You always wanted to go. You wanted to be good, so that your aunts [would] take you shopping. Then you could see kids from other places. Otherwise you were on your street, your school, your market, back to your street.

When it comes to religion, it's played a very interesting part in my life personally, but also in my family. I think Mexican Catholicism is different than Catholicism around the world. We're very, very in tune with saints. The saints are huge, at least in my family. Again, this is speaking strictly for my family. My mom to this day has an altar in their living room that has a giant cross with Jesus overlooking anything you're watching on Netflix. So, you better watch out! There's this giant cross, overlooking you and surrounded [by] two vases with angels. On top of those angels, there's two different virgins: Virgin Mary and La Virgen de Guadalupe. Most people are familiar with La Virgen de Guadalupe, but most people go, "Wait, what is that? Isn't that the same as the Virgin Mary?" To most Catholics, [they] are the same. To me, they're very different. Surrounding them are a bunch of other saints. Every single day there's, there's a different saint. In many of the calendars in Mexico, [there] is a saint of a day. For example, I grew up celebrating my birthday. I also grew up celebrating the day of my saint, or St. Joseph. I forget what day it is because I haven't celebrated that in probably twelve years. But sometime in March, my parents would bring me gifts because it was the day of my saint and you honor the saint.

The holidays we celebrate in the US are different than holidays that we celebrate in Mexico. Here we celebrate, we just celebrated Columbus Day and before that, there was another weird holiday. Those are all weird holidays to me because they're not the holidays I grew up with. May 25th, for example, is the biggest day in in our community because it's the day we honor a cross that sits at the very top of a giant mountain in our community. Across [from] it is the saint of good health. On May 25th we celebrate that saint. Everyone takes the whole week off. The government takes it off. Only grocery stores and hospitals and your immediate service needs work that day. You go to church. You go to Mass. After Mass, you walk with one of the crosses that visits one of the colonies. Then you go to the next colony, and you go to the next colony. In total, there are seven churches in our community. They're all side churches. The main one is the Basilica, as we call it. It's not really a basilica. It's a tiny, tiny church. We call it this big thing [because] it permeates everything we did.

It's not widespread across Mexico. Other communities have different days because they have different scenes. A community that was fifteen miles away from us, their big day is usually mid-April, around Easter. That's their version of our 25th. When I came to Lexington, Nebraska, there's a lot of people from that community. At our school, we all knew when it was because half the school population was gone. They all went back to Mexico to go celebrate. There was a week the teachers knew [that] all the people from that community [were] going to be gone. The kids would say, "Hey, I can't make it to soccer practice. I can't make it to speech practice because I'm going to Mexico. Why? It's las fiestas. It's the holidays."

Why does everyone love Kool-Aid [here]? We have a festival dedicated to Kool-Aid. I will never judge, but that is an impressive thing that we do in Hastings. I have become part of that. I find myself asking for days off to make sure I go to the boat races and the Kool-Aid festival, etc. I initially liked Hastings for that sense of community. Like I said, for me it's all about feeling that connection to other people. Very often, I think, people don't want to admit that we need each other. I've come to realize that part of that is because people don't want to admit that need in each other is a human thing. Instead, they view it more as a weakness, and it's not. There should be no reason why people shouldn't seek to join organizations and clubs with people who are similar to them. When it starts to get problematic is when those thoughts are negative. I'm not so much fueled on interest, but more fueled on ideologies that hurt the world that aren't filled with compassion. That's where the problem starts. The core of Hastings has that regardless of our political views, which can sometimes come up in conversations in Hastings and in our often divisive churches. There's always going to be some sort of competition between businesses, between races even. But the core of it is, most people here understand that basic reality, that we need each other. That's a culture that Hastings has that not every community has. Many communities that I've been a part of here have gotten a chance to experiment. There's one community living separately from another community. Now I find that so interesting because, even in Hastings, there is still a division between the Latino and the non-Latino communities that exist here.

When I first came to Hastings, here at the college, I felt very isolated because I had come from a place in Lexington, where I had a lot of friends who spoke both English and Spanish. I am most confident when I can speak to someone who speaks both languages. There are so many times when I think in English, and then I've got to come up with the word in Spanish to talk to a Spanish speaker, or vice versa. If I'm talking to someone who understands both, no matter what language pops into my head, it just comes out so easily and they can get more points across better.

My first day moving into the dorms I lived in Altman, which was the best dorm ever, tell everyone. Living there, it was full of English speakers. Language to me [is] really what guides what I do. I need to know first what language people are comfortable in speaking with me, and then I've got to adapt to that. When I came in, and I saw it's all English. I was scared. Here I am sitting down and the RA is going through and [saying], "All right, this person, this person. Oh, and we got a Jose is his first line, right."

Then [I say], "I'm right here."

He's like, "All right. Jose's here. Where did you leave hose B?"

Everyone dies laughing and, of course, I understand. It's meant to be a joke. I understand that, but what do you do? Your first interaction with all of these people, who now know your name, you're going to live with them for the rest of the year, go to school with them for four years, and you instantly internalize that. The quickest reaction is to laugh with them. If I stop and target him right there, no point in that. Those are things that people of color have learned to do. We have to figure out when is the right time to address, when is the time to just move on to the next thing. I started getting a lot of those things. I drove [a] van, which people [called] stereotypical. My favorite music was Mexican music. I love burritos. I can't help it.

It's just who I am. Fast forward to my first interaction [with] the community, being Walmart. I loaded up my van, which, of course, that's what you do when you [are a] first year. All the freshmen were like, "Let's take a [drive] in your van." All right let's do it. Everyone gets in my van. I take about 10 people in the van, and we make it to Walmart. We're gonna buy a futon. That's what we're there for. [We're] walking around [and] they split from the group. Right away I went over to the Mexican aisle. Stereotypical. I went there because I wanted to have hot sauce for the chips I was going to get.

Here I am looking for the hot sauce [when] this woman turns to me. She says, "Do you speak Chinese? [Do] you speak any English?"

I go, "Yes."

She goes, "Oh, thank God. I thought you were one of those people who doesn't speak English."

I was like, "Oh, no, I do."

She's like, "Can you help me? Can you tell me what this what this says on this package?"

I thought, here's this woman telling me that she's wanting to eat our food. She's wanting to partake in the culture, but then categorize us. Maybe she didn't mean to be hurtful, but in that brain of hers, she's learned to categorize non-English speaking, brown people in a certain way, and was relieved that I wasn't one of them. [What if] I said, "No, I don't speak English." What would the reaction [have been]?

That's the thing that continues to happen throughout my time in Hastings, well intentioned people with bad jokes. I don't feel like I'm the one to have to tell them, "This is how it is blah, blah, blah." Part of the reason that the Latino community isn't as connected with the non-Latino community in Hastings is possibly because the spaces are not designed for us to feel comfortable. I often think of a place in town that is. I was the only brown person I ever saw in that place. I felt so out of place in it. If I ever went back [with] one of my friends that are Freemasons and said, "Hey, we should go and have this event at this venue." [That] would not fly because they'd be, like, "Oh, hell no, let's go. Let's go instead to the auditorium. The auditorium seems like a comfortable place because it feels like it's for the whole community."

I am learning that it's not intentional. It's not this venue's fault that we don't feel comfortable. It's also not their duty to make us feel comfortable. But [it would be nice] having somebody that is constantly thinking about how their spaces would make others feel, if people become more intentional, if people stopped to think about that, and we saw things with the racial equity lens. Making it inclusive for anybody. If people stopped to think about that and made the effort, all it would take [is] wondering what the Latino people think. Call my friend Jose. "Jose, what do the Latinos think about this is this?" I go," Well, this is what I think."

It comes down to the same way that we learned to do everything in life. As [a] human, you weren't always really good at writing. You weren't always good at even writing your own name, right? But the more you did it, the easier it became. I'm to a point where now you see that you're handed a piece of paper, you see the line and you instantly know that you got to write your name on it. You don't even have to read that it says name. Subconsciously, we know how to do this. Bring people. Invite them to other spaces more often. One thing that we do in Hastings is the United by Culture festival. It's put on by the Multicultural Student Union [and] some other folks from the community. It's a place where people of diverse cultures can come and share food with each other and share entertainment with each other.

I'll tell you I was never a fan of *Seinfeld* and *Modern Family*, but we've [Latinos] got other programs. We've got our own version of *The Voice*. When everyone's talking about the voice I go, "Yeah, but did you see so-and-so came up singing the song *El Corrido*."

They're like, "What's a *Corrido*."

I'm like, "Yo and Lacombe it just what's *Lacolumbia*?"

Then people [say], "Did you hear that country song?"

And I go, "Wait, what? What country song? What?"

There's got to be a willingness from all sides to share. There also has to be the sense that when we do share something, people don't react in a way that goes, "What the heck is this?" Then the more we start to share of ourselves, and the more we start to get back that, "Oh, you're weird. It's weird." It's okay for me to talk about novellas, my favorite novella, Mexican soap operas. It's okay for me to talk about those with my roommates. It's not okay for me to talk about those at work. At work, I got to talk about *Riverdale* and the new show at New Amsterdam, and I got to talk about this other stuff. There's always those two cultures. When [I] call my mom, she has no idea what *Riverdale* is, so we talk about other stuff. I gotta stay in both cultures to keep up with the people.

It's conversations like these that I do for a living, sitting down with people who have this gut instinct to say something's wrong. Why is it that we have twenty-three Hispanic businesses, but not a single one of them goes to the chamber of commerce? Why is that? And they go, well, let's have it. Let's have a chat about that. I don't know why those twenty-three businesses don't come to your chamber of commerce. I've never been to your chamber of commerce. Let's go find out. Let's go talk to these twenty-three business owners [and] find out why they are not coming to this chamber of commerce. Then before you even say anything else, go to that chamber and say, "Have you ever invited these twenty-three businesses?" And they'll go, "Oh, yeah, we invited such and such a place." Okay. But there's twenty-two more businesses. Where are they? There's the problem.

This isn't the case in our chamber, by the way. Our chamber, here in Hastings at least, has been very, very good about showing interest in being inclusive. I went to one of their first meetings, and I was one of the only Latino people there, which was very common. It has been very common in many of the meetings that I go to. Slowly, we're starting to bring in more people. I guess that's what I do for a living, encourage those of us who understand the importance of living in this culture and learning to navigate it. There are so many little things that you have to do in this culture. Then in the Mexican culture, we go, "What the heck are they doing?" Then you switch it, and this American culture goes, "What the heck is the Mexican culture doing?" So my two cultures are clashing. I've got to be willing to invite my friends and say, "Hey, you guys, you want to come eat *mole* at my house?"

"What's *mole*? Let's find out, Honey, let's do it!"

And then vice versa.

When my mom first heard about a Kool-Aid festival, she thought, "What the heck?" When she went to her first one [she] was like, "This was really fun." Cool, awesome. Now, it's part of who we are now, as a family. What I do for a living is really figure out how we can move past these conversations. It's never easy. It's always awkward. Never easy, always awkward. So, people go, "Why the heck would I do it? Those two things don't sound fun at all." It's because they're important, and we don't always see them right away. We don't see those immediate effects. I always bring it back to my first year of college, where I joked with people joking about who I was, to not stand out, to not develop those skills. I love all of my professors. I had one professor, who, I don't believe teachers anymore, but every day would ask, "What do Latinos think about this? How would a Latino person think about this?" They kept asking me. I get it. I'm the only one in the class. But again, you're putting me in an awkward situation where I speak for everyone.

Then at one point, I went up to the professor, I said, "Hey, you know what, I'm getting really uncomfortable. This is happening every class period or, so it feels like, and it's weighing down on me because now I don't want to come to class, because I'm afraid [that] one of these days, [I'll] say something wrong."

The professor was like, "I totally understand that. And I'm so sorry that I've been putting you in that uncomfortable situation, do whatever you need to. I hope that you don't leave my class, but I guarantee that I'm going to try my best."

That openness is what I hope everybody that we come across learns. Many of my friends [back in Mexico] are still so weirded out, or they don't understand, how most of my core friend group in Hastings work on a farm. They listen to country music. They love riding horses. It's farm life. That's the life they live. But when we get together, they're my friends. Some of my best friends go, "But you're not any of those things."

I go, "I don't need to be because they're nothing like what I am. Yet we find that common ground because it comes down to that willingness and that connection that we have."

When you don't experience more interactions with people [that] have different demographics, you start to think of just the mainstream ideas. [But when you] build that connection, you start to [realize] maybe [different demographics] aren't so bad.

I am a retired special education teacher. I taught in the Hastings Public Schools for thirty-four years, and I've been retired for eight. I have lived in Hastings most of my life. I grew up here. I was born on January 16, 1953 in Banes, Cuba. My dad was working for the United Fruit Company. He was an agronomist from Nebraska. They were looking for good agronomists at United Fruit Company at that time, and so he and my mom went. He worked on sugarcane hybrids. We left before I was two, mostly because of Castro taking over. I grew up with three other siblings. We had just lots of fun with neighbor kids.

I went to school at Longfellow. Growing up was just all good memories [of the] great things that we did as a family. We lived in Lincoln for about four years, and in 1959 we moved to Hastings. I grew up here. [Upon returning to Nebraska] my dad was a banker, and my mom stayed at home and took care of us. Both my mom and my dad are from Southeast Nebraska. My dad is from Tecumseh and my mom's from Pawnee City. My dad was from a family [with]

Interviewed by Mackenzie Waltemath

ann koozer

primarily Scotland heritage. My mom's family was Czech and German. My dad's family were farmers. They were very successful farmers. My mom's father was a painter. They had lots of hard times growing up.

Both my parents were active in their churches growing up. When they moved here, they joined the First Presbyterian Church of Hastings. That's the church I grew up in. It was very important in our house. We attended church regularly, and I was always a part of the choir and children programs. Now, I would say the same thing. My husband and I are both in the same church. He also grew up Presbyterian. Our kids had to do the same thing I did. They had to go to church every Sunday, to sing in the choir, and be in all the youth groups.

I graduated from Hastings High in 1971. I went to University of Nebraska, Lincoln. I got a Bachelor of Science in education. I got degrees in music education and special education. I got my first teaching job back here in Hastings for ESU9. When I first started at ESU9, I worked mostly K-12 special education. I worked with everybody, but when I moved to Hastings Public, I did all secondary special ed. When I was at the high school, they needed somebody to work more with the kids who are not so much in the regular classroom. Although, they had been moved out into the regular classroom. The kids with learning disabilities would just come in and get help when they needed it. I got my master's degree in teaching from UNK. It was Kearney State College then, and now it is University at Kearney.

My husband was at Hastings College. He was a music education or music major. I was at UNL, and I was music major there. My parents talked about him a lot because he sang in the church choir with them. They used to talk about him all the time. They were going to set him up with my cousin. Then we were both at a music educators convention one year. We met and we talked a lot at that convention. Then he came to Lincoln and asked me to go out. My first year of teaching, when he was still a senior, we were both here. That's when we started dating seriously.

[We're] married and have two girls. Our oldest daughter is Maggie. She's 35. She lives in New York City, and she works for a big university system in the fine arts department. Our youngest daughter is Catherine, and she lives in Minneapolis. She's a Doctor of Osteopathic Medicine, and she specializes in pediatrics. When they're home, we hang out and cook. We like to travel together. We like to take vacations together, and we play tons of games. We get together at every holiday, when we can. We always have a big meal, and for Christmas we have lots of traditions. [My husband and I] taught them [the importance of] honesty, integrity, and to work hard. We did that by example more than anything, and trying to talk with them about those things. They learned a lot in school too, because character education was a big thing for them when they were in school. We always had rules they had to follow and responsibilities they had to do here.

Right after college I got a teaching job in special ed. At the time that I got a job, it was a turning point for special education services. The educational service unit here was really into putting resource teachers out into rural schools that didn't have any services for kids with learning disabilities, or any kind of challenge really. I got a job where I could get more training while I was teaching. That was a neat thing. I was, as they called them then, an itinerant resource teacher. I went to a couple of smaller towns, Giltner and Hampton. Then Robin [my husband] and I moved to Superior. I was a resource teacher there. I went to Harvard and Sandy Creek. We were trying to get services to help kids who had probably never had a whole lot of help before. I was getting training on how to do that. It was tough, but it was an exciting thing. I switched to Hastings Public after we moved back from Superior to Hastings and was a special education resource teacher. They already had a lot of special education services going in Hastings Public. I just fit in where they needed me. I was at the junior high for ten years. I was at the high school for twenty-some years.

I would work with their teachers and that kind of stuff. The kids that had a little bit more of a challenge going on, they didn't always get to go out in regular classes. So, I would have to be their reading teacher, their math teacher, whatever was appropriate for them. I liked it, but it was really tough because people, especially teachers and administrators, weren't used to those services. This all came because of change in legislation. There was a huge law called PL 94142, or something like that, that said every child was entitled to a free and appropriate education. Well, they had challenges. What was appropriate for them was not always the same as everybody else. That's why all of this started. That was the hard part, trying to educate teachers and administrators as well as working with students.

In my spare time, I volunteer a lot. I'm on a couple of boards in town. I am on an advisory board for Goodwill. They serve people with all kinds of disabilities. I'm very interested in music. I would say cooking is a hobby of mine. I hang out with some of my old friends and read and just do stuff here at home. I volunteer at church and the museum. I'm on the Hastings Museum board. It used to be more of a governing board, but now the city switched it to an advisory board. I still love that. I'm on the Hastings Public Schools Foundation Board, and we help to raise money for the public schools.

I have Multiple Sclerosis [MS]. That's when your body attacks itself and destroys the myelin that is around nerve cells. It makes its connections between nerves. It disrupts that connection in a lot of different areas. I was diagnosed in 1996. It took a long time, and I had several MRIs, even one that was totally clear. I went to the Mayo Clinic and they said, "Everything's fine. We don't know the problem." At the beginning, my legs would fall asleep while I was walking, like when your legs fall asleep being in a position too long. My legs would do that when I was working or walking down the hall at school. I went to get checked out, but they just said [it] may be a pinched nerve or something. I'd say it took probably several months. I have a lot of sensory issues. One of my legs feels like it's numb on the inside. I have a lot of tingling sensation in both my arms and my legs. I have a leg that's very weak. I have fatigue issues, huge issues with fatigue and stamina, and being able to walk long distances. I can't do it. Compared to somebody else who might be in a wheelchair, I'm very lucky. I'm okay with it. I am, just because I'm so lucky. It's not obvious that I have something wrong. On the other side of that, because it doesn't look like I have anything wrong, I think it's hard for some people to understand why I don't do this, or why I can't do certain things, or I just choose not to.

It just depends on the day, and it depends on how hot it is, with fatigue issues, and how much I can get done. I always have lots of things I need to get done, but if I don't feel like it, or don't have the energy, I just can't do it. If I want to go in and cook something or do a big meal, I just can't do that without having to stop and sit down for a while. I can't always get done what I want to get done. Especially lately, I've had some balance issues. I must really be careful. I must go a lot slower than I ever did. I must always be mindful if the ground is uneven and I must hang onto somebody or something. I can't shop for hours, like somebody else might be able to. People will ask me how I'm doing because they always say, "Well, you look fine." I'll say I'm doing okay, but I don't explain it a lot.

I have lots of friends who were very upbeat, and Robin was very supportive and just said, "You know you can do this." I decided for myself that I had to. I couldn't think about all the bad things that might happen. I just stopped thinking about them. At first, it's a crushing blow. You just don't know what's going to happen. For my family it wasn't easy, because none of us knew what was going to happen. I think we were all a little bit on edge and a lot of things would come up. I probably didn't deal with them the best, but they were always very supportive, especially my friends at school and my family. People in the beginning would always say they were praying for me, and I felt that. It's carried me through for sure. My own faith has, but the faith of others has too, as far as giving me strength and being able to carry on.

I try to be supportive if I hear somebody's been newly diagnosed. If I know them, I'll try to be a support system for them too. I feel like people don't know the spectrum of MS. I think they just assume things are going to be bad for you someday. That may not be true. They just assume you're going to be totally incapacitated. They don't know that it's not always that way. I've seen that, especially since I taught kids with disabilities. I see firsthand what they're doing and how they talk about being out in the community, and how welcoming everyone is. I know tons of businesses that will take people, students or kids, out of school for a job experience. I think people are very good about including them.

Hastings is a small city. It's very homey. The people are nice. Most of the time, I think it's a nice place to live. It's safe. There's lots of things going on, especially in the arts. It has a very good public school educational system. I think the college adds a lot to the community. There's certain things that are hard. We must drive to get to fly anywhere. We must drive to see big major art things, but I do like it. It's very comfortable. It's very predictable. I mean, it's not stressful. I think that you can pretty much do what you want to do and you're safe. You can get where you want to go without spending a lot of time traveling. I can get where I want to in five minutes.

chris langenberg

Interviewed by Cornelius Barber

I am from right here in Hastings, Nebraska. I was born and raised in central Nebraska. I have [my] bachelor's in human services from Doane College and then [my] master's in public health from the University of Creighton.

I work at Cookout Rivals. I've been job hunting, but I like Rivals a lot. From the bottom of my heart, I actually ended up staying with Rivals because I like the people that work there. I really liked the management. The bosses that I worked for are some of the best bosses I've ever had. The more I've worked at Rivals, the more I've realized there is this generation out there that is accepting of queer people. I like to call myself queer because it feels comfortable. They're not biased against me. It's one of those jobs where it's okay to be myself. [I'm] comfortable with everybody. I can come to work not having to worry about what people think and all the other crazy, stupid stuff.

[Considering if the LGBT community is treated fairly in Hastings, it] depends on who you're dealing with. The last school board meeting really revealed that there are still people here, people who claim to be devout Christians and people in the professional workforce, who still claim that we're mentally ill. We have a very wide mixture in terms of demographics. Hastings is much divided politically between Democrats and Republicans. It's the younger generation [that is] more okay with LGBT people in this town. Whereas the professionals, the people that have been here long term or the older generations, are still not [accepting]. [The] LGBT community has to fight for our space here in Hastings a lot more.

I don't think [the LGBT community is treated equally in the workforce]. I can tell you why. You hear stories. You hear the rumors. One of the people that I knew who was openly gay and considered [him and his partner] married [had to deal with it]. He was working as the director of [an organization] here in town, and rumor has it that he was fired from that job because he was overt. [This] was about five or six years ago. It's not just in the professional world. It's anything else where they say you can't be racist, [but] you can be sexist. I don't think that jobs are quite on board [with] discrimination against gay people. There's no videos people are watching in the workplace [on it]. You watch your videos on sexual harassment or sex discrimination against women versus men. You have to watch those videos when you go through job training, but being part of LGBT is not brought up.

There was one story I heard that sounds crazy. It happens all the time where there was a flamboyantly gay male working in an organization around here and that particular individual was treated nice to his face. They would come up and ask him about himself, etc. Behind his back, it was the complete opposite. It was people going and reporting him [because] they were offended by [what he was telling them when they asked]. That's the kind of discrimination that exists in the workplace. Everywhere you go. Everywhere. [For] LGBT people, especially here in central Nebraska, it's, "I want to act nice to your face. I want to pretend that I like you to make it look good, but behind your back I'm okay with talking bad about you to the higher ups." It's an institutional type of discrimination because it's protected by the institution within.

I myself haven't had as [many] problems, unless I was to go out wearing lipstick, painted nails, or differently dressed than the norm. [That] might make it even more troublesome. It depends on how you can blend in. People are still expecting these gender norms not to be crossed anywhere. People are expecting women to behave as stereotypical women, [with strictly] female behaviors. People are expected to play gender roles. They're expected to play these stereotypical versions and when those expectations aren't met socially, when you see gay people, different people, people who are more flamboyant, then it's harder for them to blend in. You get treated differently because of it.

The most offensive thing I find is people that think we're mentally ill or some kind of social deviance. I've been more recently offended by [what I] see on social media. There's been fake news everywhere that the LGBT community is trying to [bring] in pedophiles. That's a deep thing to bring up, but that's offensive to me right there. I don't know why anybody would think that I would want [to be a pedophile]. I've never met any LGBTQ [group] who wants people who are committing harm to other people to be encouraged to join that community. But there are people out there that believe that. On the other side, there are people that are so homophobic. They throw out words like *faggot*, that horrible bomb. They think that we're mentally ill or a social deviant that's going straight to hell because that's their religion. That's what they were raised to believe in. That is not right.

I feel I've been treated differently because of [my] sexual orientation. Sometimes I can't think of any super, strong examples off the top of my head, but it depends on how well I was blending in with everyone else. If I was just talking about sports, didn't do anything, and my appearance wasn't out of the ordinary from what is expected in the social cultural norm, then people may not look at me. Everything you say or anything you do that goes against that norm [is revealing]. If I started telling people, [in my] career those things about me, then I do think that they would treat me differently.

If people knew I was gay, they would look at me differently in the hiring process. Absolutely. I try not to bring that kind of conversation up [during the hiring process]. I applied at an HIV clinic and one of the bosses that interviewed me was gay, but I was not comfortable in telling him that I'm queer. I was not comfortable even at that point. That's weird to think of it that way. Being openly gay and going towards jobs with people that [are as well], you would think that that would be the opposite. Of course they're not going to tell you, "Sorry, we didn't hire you because you're gay or you're transgender."

That was my most recent experience. The other place I work at, I feel they would definitely not [have] hired me if I came forward and directly said, "I'm gay." They would not want to hire me, but they would find other reasons to disqualify me. [They'd] say, "Well, he doesn't have enough experience. We just didn't feel like he was the right fit for our organization." It's little things like that. They just beat around the bush.

If they [hired you] and found out six or nine months later, [they'd say], "Yeah, he's a hard worker, but he's flamboyantly gay or he does these things outside of work that we think [are] unprofessional." They could turn around and say, "Your performance isn't satisfactory to us anymore. We just don't think you're a good fit." Then they can let you go without giving a reason. They don't have to give a reason. Welcome to Republicanism.

If I had to define [discrimination], I would [say] it's the prejudicial treatment of somebody else based on who they are, whether it be their race, their gender, or their sexual orientation. I would define discrimination [with] examples. It's what's swept under the rug in workplaces and in professional places, professional spaces. With the LGBTQ community, they would sweep it under the rug [and say], "We don't have that here." It's people who find out who you are, and personally they may act like they're okay with it, but behind your back they're [not]. It's the rumors.

I don't think the city of Hastings or the state of Nebraska is doing anything to improve relations between LGBTQ people and other people. The governor isn't the most supportive, but I don't want to just blame him. Put it this way, I think a great example of that is when I went to a health department meeting a while back, in Lincoln. Nebraska is strongly conservative about the LGBTQ community. An issue was brought up that in the state, it was STI and HIV testing they were looking at, and I was doing a project for my public health degree. Somebody said we needed to go to the communications department at DHS and ask to put billboards out in the state, all the way from North Platte to Kearney and then all the way up into Omaha and Lincoln areas. DHS was the chain of communication [and it] got brought back to them that, "This isn't something that would be accepted by our state government right now." We have to have this approved by our state legislature and the people at the state. If the state government says, "We don't want this, and we don't approve of these messages being sent out to the public mass media," [then we couldn't]. So, no. The state's not doing anything right now to promote better relationships. They never will if we keep voting for prejudiced people.

I can't say that I'm in a position of leadership, but I want to say there's power in numbers, even in Nebraska. Right now, the LGBTQ community seems like a small community, but we're not. We're all over the place. Our biggest issue that we face right now is [that] we're divided amongst ourselves. Inner-circle drama, it's there. Instead of being divided amongst ourselves about the drama going on in our own community, we have to come together regardless of our personal differences and start forming that alliance. We are a community of LGBTQ people, queer people, whatever we want to call ourselves, and we need to, need to have that voice. We need people that want to come forward and stand up. [We need] the leadership to go forward and push ourselves. We have individuals like that who are trying. Brandi [Bosier] is transgender here in Hastings. Brandi and her partner are some of the most visible LGBTQ persons in this community. She's openly transgender, and she's not afraid to say it. That lack of fear, of consequences, is something that we need more of. We are not going to get anywhere unless we have power in numbers, unless we have people that are backing us, and we have allies.

I am originally from Guadalajara, Mexico. I was raised with the nuns. I was at a boarding school. My mom came to the United States when I was at the age of three, and she was a single parent. She had to raise five kids, and she would send money to Mexico. I came from a family of four girls and one boy. My dad, I really don't know much about him. He passed away when I was three years old. [My mom] came to [the] United States, and then she went back to Mexico. Then my brother was born, and we came too. She brought us to Waterloo, Iowa. Waterloo is my hometown. I grew up in a Mexican restaurant. When we came to United States [we] were [the] only Hispanic girls and a boy at Waterloo Public Schools. Waterloo is about as big as Hastings and Grand Island [combined]. I have my mom and two sisters there. And that's where I met my ex-husband. I met my [ex-]husband in Iowa when I was twenty-one. Then in 1990 I had my daughter, Desiree. She lives in Colorado. We moved to Sandusky, Ohio, and we lived there for three years. When we went to Ohio, I had to take my driver's license. At age

Interviewed by Kaelan Dae

raquel maar

twenty-eight, I got my driver's license. I had to because it was a smaller town than what I was used to. Then we moved to Pennsylvania. Then from Pennsylvania, we moved to Nebraska. In 1996, I had my son DJ.

When he was two years old, we moved to Hastings, in June of 1998. I started working for Hastings Public Schools as a peer educator for ESL. That's [when] I got involved with a lot of the Hispanic community. I met one of the police officers, and they [asked] if I wanted to interpret [for] them. [I] finally got involved with that in 1999 and started interpreting for the police department. When they need an interpreter, I'm the one who gets called to go in. I started earning the respect in the community, and I was doing a lot more then. At the time, I didn't have my GED or my high school diploma. I went to CCC and got my GED. One of the teachers that I work with, Mary Lampkin, her husband was the chief of police for [the] Grand Island Police Department. She was my mentor. She's the one that buil[t] my self-esteem. Because of her, I start believing that I could do more, that I can provide better for my kids. Then I started working more for the schools and getting involved with the community. It opened more doors for me.

I got a job offer [from the] Department of Health and Human Services [as an] economic assistance social worker. I started as a trainee worker because for that kind of job you need a college degree. [As a trainee], I can be trained and then get promoted. I didn't have to go to college for that. I worked for Department of Health and Human Services for twelve years and then I got involved again more with the community. There was a child in 2006 that passed away [from] leukemia, and [the] parents didn't speak English. I got involved with the arrangements. Ever since then, I'm the one who gets called to do funeral arrangements. Apparently, the word just got out of me helping at the Department of Health and Human Services. I became a social worker for the Hispanic community. Back then, we didn't have the call centers, so I had a caseload of 400. I try to help people the [most] I can. Then I found my job with Walmart. I was working at Walmart and then I got to know more people there. And working with that police department and all, I just get so involved in the community. A lot of the people that I know, clients and people that know me work [or] live in the trailer court so they know where I live. Whenever they need help with something, they just come over here or they call me.

    My hopes were to teach my kids a better life. I hope I will never raise my kids the same way I was raised. I have better dreams for my kids. I swore they will never be raised like I was. I told my ex-husband I didn't want to move again, and Hastings became home for the kids. It seemed like a nice small town to raise kids. I got involved with my kids' activities all the time and always my schedule was around my kids'. Growing up, I always got them involved in everything. I always supported my kids on everything they did. I believe that education is big. I help with the schools. I still do interpreting for the schools even though I don't work anymore, but whenever they need me to interpret, I do so. I started working for the county attorney's office. I'm trying to get my certification for interpreting. The county attorney's office can help me advance on my interpreting certifications.

Most of my best friends are American people because we were the only Hispanic girls at the school. I think that was easier back then, because nowadays when you see the schools have more of the Hispanic population in it, more of the Hispanics stick together. I don't know if you ever see that, but Hispanic kids stay together. To me that's wrong because we should be all [be] mingling with [each] other, not defining each other as Hispanic and white people. It is hard for me because I was married to an American person. My kids are half white, half Mexican. Nowadays you see on TV more of that separation of cultures. I don't judge. My mom taught us there's no word such as discrimination. I don't believe in discrimination, I believe that you work hard for what you earn and if you don't you need to try harder. I never really felt discriminated [against]. My best friends are American, and I do have a few friends that are Hispanic. I [have] this Hispanic family that I helped three or five years ago. Their little boy passed away, and I helped with funeral arrangements. Since, this mother had two more kids and I was present for the birth of their children. Those children call me Nana, and they're Hispanic, and I love them like they were my own family. I don't believe that there is such [a] thing as discrimination. I think a lot of that discrimination partly comes from the media making it sound like Hispanics and Americans need to be separated.

When I was thirteen, I didn't want to come to the United States. Again, it was a lot because of the relationship I have with my mom. To me, my mom was a stranger. I didn't know what I was expecting [in] the United States. When we came, we didn't speak English. We hated it. I hated because we [could not] understand each other and stuff like that. Then it came to the point that we had to learn English. I thank my mother for that effort and for the sacrifices that she made. Because of her, we all became somebody. She believed in us, that we could do better.

Our community. I say Hastings is very welcoming. If you need something, you just need to ask. The Chamber of Commerce will help. You can go to the churches. I think Hastings is a very welcoming community. We will make it easier for people that move from other states. The best thing is how involved we can get, how can we get people involved. Hastings wants to grow. Hastings wants to make our communities safe for our children. That's the best part of it. They concentrate on the children. I believe that our teachers work very hard to make our kids be successful. Without our teachers they wouldn't be a community. They get so involved. I like Nebraska. It's my home.

I was talking to my son and my daughter the other day, because they came for a wedding.

I don't listen to politics because you can never win in politics. You can never say the right thing or do the right thing or say or vote for the right president. I tell people I'm undecided on that. I'm not Democrat or Republican. I keep that to myself. When I became a US citizen, it was a thing that I had to have. I came illegally to the United States. My mom brought us into the United States. She brought us visitors, but we never went back. My mom married an American and she started working on immigration papers for us, but at the age of eighteen, she could not work on my immigration papers. I was ahead of age. My mom wanted to pay somebody to marry me so I can work on my immigration papers. I told my mom at that time that I will not marry for that. That became a big issue with my mom and me. I got amnesty in 1986 I believe. That's when I worked on my immigration papers. A lady that used to babysit said she called immigration. Back then, [you] used to be able to just call immigration and they will answer. You [didn't] talk to a machine. The lady that was at the immigration office felt compelled about my story, and she told the lady that used to babysit to make contact with this gentleman. His name was Joe Featherston. I will never forget that name because he was the one that helped me and told me what I needed to do to work on my immigration papers. He told me step-by-step what I needed to do. I was supposed to meet him at a restaurant. Here is an eighteen-year-old that didn't know nothing about this guy. We were meeting at a restaurant, and I didn't tell my mom about it because my mom and I were not talking to each other. He was a very nice guy. He told me what I needed to do file paperwork. Back then to file for my paperwork, it cost me almost $1,000. By the time I met my ex, I already had my authorization to work.

I still have [the] pay stub of my first paycheck that ever they took taxes [on]. It was $87, and I was very proud of that. Then when I was eight months pregnant with my daughter Desiree, I got my residence. When I became a US citizen, I was pregnant with DJ, and it came to the point that I never thought somebody will discriminate [against] me because I get along with everybody. I am friends with everybody. I'm very social. I was telling my kids the other day, all [my] years in the United States, I never felt discriminated [against].

On Tuesdays and Thursdays, I work at the Holiday Inn as a hostess. I serve wine and beer and never, ever has anybody treated me [as if I was] below them. I was always treated equal. I was telling them [my children], that this woman came in and out of nowhere, and I thought she was kidding, she goes *"Una Cervesa por favor."* I'm like okay, maybe she's just trying to practice on her Spanish. Then for a wine and *beno,* she goes *"rapido."* I'm like, you did not talk to me like that.

I said, "I'm sorry ma'am, but I do speak English."

[She said,] "Well you're not moving fast enough, so *rapido.*"

I [thought] holy crap. Then she starts talking to the [other] woman about slow service, when the beer and wine is free at the Holiday Inn if you are a guest. The woman just kept staring me up and down, and I was, like, "What is her problem?" That was the first time I ever felt like the woman was trying to feel [as if she was] better than me. Just because you work at a hotel and you're Hispanic, that doesn't mean you don't speak English. She just assumed that I didn't speak English.

Then even her friend [said], "You did not do that."

And then there was my regular and there was some guy that goes like, "Did she just talk to you like that?"

I said, "I think so."

He goes, "Some people can be so rude."

I came home, and I was telling my kids about it. That was the first time I really felt discriminated [against], just because she thought she could get away with things.

My daughter is moving back to Hastings, Nebraska. I kept the house because this is home for my kids. Their friends are here. My mom, my ex, and his parents are in Iowa. [Still,] my kids feel that this is home. I kept the house because of them. I wanted them to have a home to come to. Hastings is closer than Waterloo for my daughter. Omaha is only two and a half hours away. It's easier for DJ to come here. Plus, we have a lot of friends that my kids grew up with. They're like family. That's what keeps me here. Plus, my job, of course. I love my job.

I believe the person you are will follow you. I just love my community. I love Hastings. I really do. I mean, I wish I could do more, but I don't have enough hours in the day to do it. Right now, it's hard because I'm working three jobs until my daughter moves back in.

I'm close to achieving the American dream. I got a bucket list. I want to finish my bucket list. Once I finish my bucket list, I have achieved everything. If I can achieve to live until I'm 100 years old, then I have lived the American dream. The American Dream is all about your blessings, what you have in life now. I believe that you can be anything you want. You just [have] to put your mind to it.

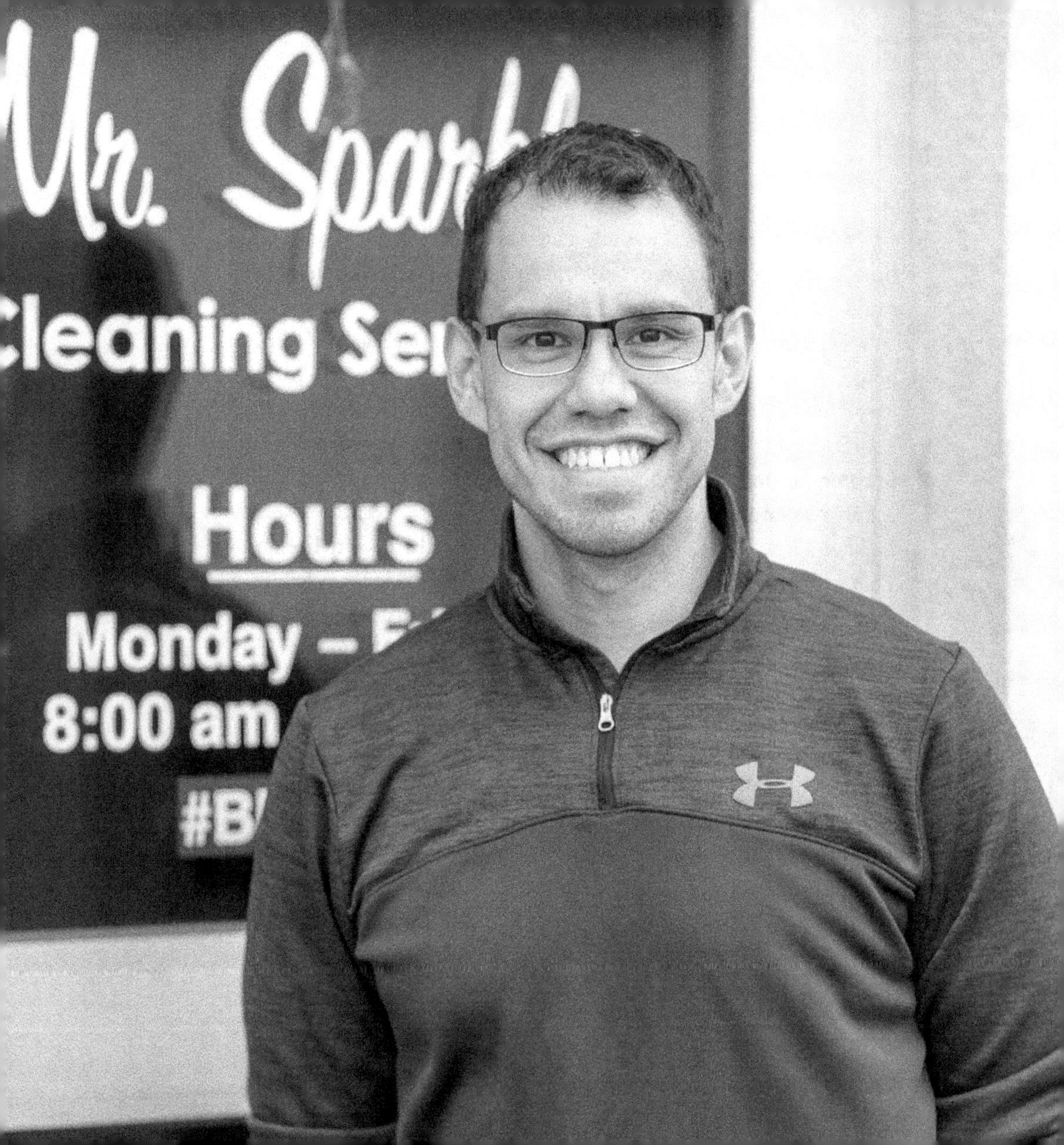
Mr.
Cleaning
Hours
Monday –
8:00 am

My name is Carlos Magallanes. I always go by Gus; that's my middle name. I am thirty-seven years old. I moved to Hastings in 2000, right after I turned eighteen years old. I came here to America illegally and it's been an adventure. I believe I've been in Hastings for eighteen or nineteen years, and I love this town. I co-own a business with my partner Wayne. We own a cleaning business here in Hastings called Mr. Sparkles Home and Cleaning Services, and everything is going great.

I was born in Mexico, Guadalajara. It's the second biggest city in Mexico. My mom is still living there in Mexico. She is sixty-nine years old. My dad died of alcoholism when I was fourteen years old. I grew up going to a Catholic church every Sunday. I had my First Communion, Confirmation, and all of that. That's one of the reasons I was so confused on my sexuality because [God] was, like, "No, this is a sin." That gets in your head. My schooling in Mexico was a challenge because I was bullied every day. I didn't really hang out with anybody. I didn't have any friends. Every time I

carlos (gus) magallanes

Interviewed by Paul Erickson

tried to make friends anywhere, they would say "Oh, he's gay," or "He's a faggot." That made my life miserable and that's why I knew [school] was not for me. I just finished middle school and that was it for me. I don't want to go to school anymore.

    I made the decision to come to America when I was eighteen years old because I was confused about my identity and my sexuality. I knew I needed to do something about this because I could not keep on living that way. I was confused about what I wanted and what I wanted to look like. I had an opportunity to come to America. A friend of mine was like, "You should come, life is better here than in Mexico." In Mexico I was making around $3 per week and only had one day off in the middle of the week. My friend was, like, "I'm going to help you. Let's do this together." We came in the car and we were driving through Cuidad Juarez to the borderline. My friend said to me, "I hope they don't stop us." Sometimes they just ask, "Where are you going?" and then say, "Welcome to America, go ahead." Sometimes they stop you, ask for registration, who is inside the car, and everything. The guard asked us to stop and then [my friend was] like, "Just let me handle this. It's going to be okay." They asked her to roll the window down and they asked her, "Can you give me your registration?" She gave them the registration from the car and they were, like, "Are you a resident or an American citizen?" and she replied, "I'm an American citizen." They were, like, "Okay, can you show me your birth certificate?" [That] made her nervous and she's, like, "Oh, it's in the trunk." She had to get out again and check. Another agent came to my window and I was, like, "Oh, no" in my head. He knocked on the window and gives me the sign to roll the window down. Back then I didn't speak English; zero; nothing. He told me to roll the window down. I rolled down the window and I absolutely, even up to today, don't know what he asked me. But he asked me something and all I said was, "Oh, yeah, of course." He was, like, "Welcome to America." I thought, "Whoa. That was easy."

Sometimes people ask me, "Did you go to school?" or "How did you learn to speak English?" A lot of people don't know this about me, but one of the ways I learned English is by watching Oprah. I would put the subtitles on and I would just watch and read. Little by little you start getting it. I'm not saying that is perfect. But it worked for me.

My full-time job is in Grand Island at Hornady Manufacturing. They make ammunition and bullets. Wayne and I started our business with $100 to buy cleaning supplies. We started cleaning restaurants and little by little we grew. Now we have up to 160 employees. Wayne is more of a silent partner because he has the business mind. I do the work end of it. He started working because we weren't making a lot of money.

When you open with nothing, with no investors or savings accounts, all the money we make goes back into the business. Sometimes we clean for free for people who are going through cancer and different things. We try to continue to build. We're going to grow our business and keep going until he can quit his job. Then we'll both own it ten years from now: probably seventy.

I have a part-time job at the YMCA. I teach yoga and high-intensity cardio class. On the weekends I teach CrossFit at the center in town by the mall. We're always on the go. I also exercise and take care of our dogs.

I met Wayne through Facebook about five years ago. We just got out of bumpy, bad relationships. We were having a conversation and we both thought, "This is going somewhere."

Wayne thinks I was looking for a partner that has family values because we were both married to women before and we have children. Wayne's boys are thirteen and ten years old, and my daughter is ten years old. That led to a different life. A lot of people just assume gay people have these wild crazy senseless lives. Some of us want to have a serious relationship or a family just like everybody else. That's why we started talking. It's fresh out of the closet, kids, and finally coming to terms with who we were. It's still a process living in Hastings, trying to run a business and prove that you're just as good as everybody else. People kind of look down on us at times or people feel uncomfortable or awkward around us because of our sexuality. It's silly because that shouldn't be the first thing you think when you meet somebody. I don't assume anybody is straight or gay when I look at them. I just look at [them] as a person. Sometimes we have issues in town with it. Being together helps. We've done great things in the community compared to a lot of people.

I enjoy living in Hastings. We have some ups and downs with some people. The state of Nebraska is highly conservative. There are democratic people and open-minded people in small parts of the town. I like living here. This is my hometown. I have pretty much lived half my life here in Hastings. I know it's a small town, but I love it here. The best thing about Hastings is the growing diversity. It's taking baby steps, but you can see that there's more diversity, different cultures, different colors, and different sexualities.

julie mcdougal

Interviewed by Alex Rieflin

I grew up in Pawnee City, which is down in southeastern part of Nebraska. My husband was from Tecumseh, which is about twenty miles north. We both live in southeast Nebraska and we both worked on the staff at the university. I grew up in a family with five brothers and a sister. I had four older brothers. When I was little, we lived across the line into Kansas. I was born in Kansas, but then we moved to Pawnee County. When they changed the line of the town, we had to move from the city school to the town school because we were about two miles from town. I finished eighth grade in town. I learned more in the country schools but then I went to Pawnee City High.

We did not have a lot of money. My oldest brother was a farmer; he stayed, and he took care of the farm. The second brother was a country school teacher and he saved money for my third brother to go to the university. Dick went to the university and graduated. Wayne had all these plans about going to college himself but World War Two came. All the boys disappeared [into the war] except my oldest brother who stayed home to tend to the farm. I graduated from high school during the war. I went to the University of Nebraska during the war, graduated in 1946, and it was a quiet time as far as students are concerned. When I was in college, I worked for the state's 4-H Club Office every summer for three summers. We traveled, and I lead the singing. That's why I was hired. I majored in home economics and after I graduated I taught home economics. After I'd been teaching, I came back and worked in the Four-H office, at the university until Jim and I were married. Then we moved to Cuba.

During that time, Battista was the ruler; he had taken over about the day we got there. We went down on a ship and when we get off the ship by the state capital there was a little boy sitting there. He reached from behind and took my purse and my husband said, "What's he doing?" I said, "Oh, he has taken my purse." Jim took off after the little boy and he had jumped on a bus. Jim jumped on the bus and the kid jumped off and Jim tackled him on the capital lawn. Jim got my purse back because I had a check for $5,000 and it was all the money we had in the world. Whilst in Cuba, Jim worked for United Fruit Sugar Company where he was an agronomist. We were in Cuba when our oldest daughter was born and when it was time for our second daughter to be born, I said, "Let's go home."

We decided to come back, and Jim was going to go into business. We were going to live in Lincoln. The fellow that Jim was going into business with drove to Plasmith to get a car. He had [an accident] and was killed. There we were sitting in Lincoln. Jim worked with a family for a year. They were in commercial work, but I can't tell you much about that. After working for the family for a year, Jim said, "No more." He said, "It's too complicated with a family try to keep up the business." One of his friends said there was a bank in Hastings, looking for an Ag man. In 1957, Jim decided that he would take this job with the bank in Hastings. He had always, ever since he came to work in Hastings, had liked it. We all like Hastings, very much. Women always said, "[Hastings was] a good place to raise a family." We found that to be true.

Our children grew up here, and we were always satisfied with the surrounding schools. My oldest daughter said, "If [we were] in another town I might go [to college] but I'm not." Our son went to Hastings College. The college was always well thought of by the people who live here and many people who knew about it. We've always been very happy with the Presbyterian Church. Jim served on the Board [of Trustees] of Hastings College and he was a good friend of Tom Reeves, who was a president of Hastings College. One of mine is a graduate of Wesleyan. My youngest daughter is a business manager for a company in Des

Moines, and she was a very good student and she has a very good job. My oldest daughter married a Hastings College boy who has taught at Hastings College. My second daughter married a teacher as well; they live in Colorado in Greeley.

    Hastings could be more outgoing and more inclusive of people but it's a pretty good place. Not much has changed over the years, not in my world because I don't get out, especially not lately. I haven't been out a lot since my husband died, and so I don't have a connection. He was in the banking business, and I know Hastings prided itself on banks that were locally owned. I suppose it's gotten to be a little bit more of a larger community and we don't have the same feeling as a smaller community as before.

I like being a middle child; it's cool. It definitely has pros and cons. My sister [Mikaelah], who's the other middle child, we're just so close. Growing up and having a sister as your best friend was a lot different than having a brother or a best friend who was another boy. I got to see things from a female side. When I was first starting to date, she gave me a girl's perspective that a lot of people don't really get. [Mateo] is two years older than I am. He taught me how to not do things. Sometimes, one of the best ways to learn is showing you what not to do. That's what I appreciate. He was the firstborn, so he was going through everything for the first time. I was watching him experience some stuff. It was also cool because I got to be a leader for my younger siblings, Ethan and Michaela, who both go to school here.

  I was born and raised in California for five years. I left because my mom was from Connecticut. It was pretty conservative. It was cool. We stayed there for six years. Then we went back to California for seven months. The cost of living [in California] is so high, so

Interviewed by Kaeden Markham

casey molifua

we were all living in one room, the six of us. We were staying in the extra room of [someone else's] really nice house. It was cool that they let two parents and four kids run around in a pretty nice house.

Then my dad got a job offer in Missouri. On our road trip across the country, we stopped in Nebraska. My dad's job fell through in Missouri. We decided to stay [in Nebraska]. We found a rental home in Lincoln. We came in my sixth-grade year. I went to Goodrich Middle School in Lincoln. I walked to and from school every day. My mom didn't want me to do high school in California. There's a lot more temptation, opportunities to get in trouble. My mom tells me I always wanted to have perfect attendance in elementary school, but in high school I didn't [care]. My middle school experience in Lincoln was a wake-up call. It was crazy diverse. I was [exposed] to a lot of new things, such as drugs, alcohol, and bullying. I got suspended every year in middle school for stupid stuff. Middle school was crazy, but I wouldn't change it.

When I first came to Hastings, it was the first time I attended school by myself. That experience [was] brand new to me. Then my sister came here right afterwards. Even after serving at Guantanamo Bay, Ethan came to Hastings. It was cool [that] they wanted to follow in my footsteps. It's cool creating our own legacy. I was following the tail of our brother, Mikaelah followed me, and Ethan followed her. I was gaining some success here and I was enjoying this community. I like the quietness of Nebraska.

When I first came to Hastings, there were five black guys on the football team, two Polynesian guys, myself, and then another Samoan kid named Marcus Moore. Under the surface, I definitely think there was some racism or bigotry there, but I never saw it first-hand until my buddy Joe came from Tuco, California. He's another Polynesian guy. When a Polynesian sees another Polynesian it's automatically a little love. I took him out to Walmart and Taco Bell. We were waiting for our food and there was a little girl in there. She kept looking at Joe and his full sleeve tattoo [that] is in his language. She looked curious and asked her mom, "Why is their skin so tan?" I can't forget what her mother said, "You're white, and that's what makes you special." Thinking back about it, I wish I would have [said something]. That could have been a really big teaching moment for her daughter.

I'm half Caucasian. My mom is Irish, Italian, German, and Swedish. I have to remind myself that I'm mixed even though I have tan skin and Polynesian tribal tattoos on my arm. People look [at those who are different]. That's just the nature of human beings. I get looked at a little bit weird because of Islamophobia. I have tan skin [and] a big black beard, [so] some people mistake me for Middle Eastern. There's some people who ask what ethnicity you are. I actually like that question because it opens up a line of communication. [They] care enough to know what makes me ... me.

The toughest moments growing up [were] from a financial standpoint. This really hurt my parents too. My mom always [said], "I wish I could financially provide for you better." We moved a lot. We had always been in low-income housing growing up. J.Cole said, "Even though sometimes we had less compared to some brothers down the block, man, we was blessed." I think about that. Financially we were never rich, but I always had the strongest support system ever. My mom is my biggest rock. I played clarinet [in] fifth grade when I lived in Connecticut. My dad was at my recital. He's this six foot, 350 pound, old guy coming to watch his son play clarinet. That was special to me. I didn't have the money but I always was rich in relationships and family. I wouldn't trade that support system for nice cars, a nice house, [or a] nice neighborhood. I wouldn't trade that for the world.

Right before I graduated high school, my dad suffered a stroke and aneurysm. That really took a toll on my family. My dad became handicap. He was in ICU [for] six weeks. [We] didn't really know what was going to happen to my dad and I [was] going off to college in two months to play college football. This was my dad's dream. He wanted me to graduate college. My older brother dropped out of Morningside after a year and a half. So, I felt like it was my responsibility. We had never had somebody go to college and I just thought, "I'm going to do this."

For me, the hardest part of college was leaving home. I was independent and I was going to school for the first time by myself. I [couldn't] just go down the hallway of the high school and see my little sister [or] my little brother. I was an independent for the first time, which was tough. I remember sitting up in my room [and] crying myself to sleep some nights. I felt so bad because I just left my mom there with my little brother [and] sister, dealing with my dad. My mom's tough. My dad ended up surviving [and] coming out of the hospital, but he was not the same. He couldn't speak. His health wasn't great. [It was] a really hard transition for my entire family. Then for me to just up and leave like that was hard to me. Deep down I knew that I had to do this. I had to make that sacrifice.

I thought about quitting, especially my first year. I had this deep thing that was going on with me that I didn't want to share with anybody because it was hard. I didn't know how to cope with it. So, I was coping with it the wrong ways: partying, drug and alcohol abuse, just not doing the things I needed to do. Looking back at it, I see the students that I work with. I see that they're hurting too. Deep down there's something that's making them respond and behave the way that they're behaving. I know exactly what that's like.

I just had to find two or three people. I was, like, "Bro, you gotta keep me here. You have to keep me here." Once Mikaelah came here, it became a lot easier. I love [being] independent, [but] when my sister came here I said, "Okay, I have another purpose. I can't leave my sister." If I would have left, I wouldn't have started this legacy. This whole community is something special. Something's going on here. I don't know what it is yet, but I'm so happy to be a part of it.

I'm here for a reason. I'm really trying to be present where I am right now. I know I'm not gonna be here the rest of my life, but this is where I am right now. I might as well make the best of it. Ever since I started my master's program, I really started to learn. My goal is to get my doctorate in education. I'm gonna go get my EDS, which is an educational specialist. I really enjoy leadership motivation. My goal is to get my doctorate by the time I am thirty. I'm twenty-five right now.

One of my goals is to remain physically fit. I don't want to be washed up. I'm stronger now. I really like weightlifting and strength training. At some point I would love to get married and have a family. I want to be a good father, but that is down the road. One of my dreams is to be a motivational speaker and writ[e] a book, telling my story and encouraging people. I want to tell the younger generation that it is okay to fail because I have failed so many times. I've learned more from failing than success. Take risks. It doesn't have to be perfect. Don't think about it, just do it. Authenticate yourself. Self empowerment, self happiness, [and] self love [are so important]. This is my life and I'm thinking about the right now. I'm figuring stuff out and I'm growing so much every year.

Every single year that I've been here, the food has gotten better. I've been here eight years. My favorite place to eat is Russ's. I thought it was just a grocery store, but there's a little cafe. It's easily my favorite place to eat. There are taco trucks on different streets. [We] have the luxury of authentic Mexican food. A Chick-fil-A should open up here. They'd get a lot of business. They don't open up on Sundays because they're Christian. They would thrive out here. When Dunkin' Donuts opened up there was a huge line. When it comes to food, I'm a garbage disposal. I love a good homemade meal, though. Three years ago my dad told me he was going to come teach me a family lasagna recipe. That's pretty special. He's [telling me] this stuff and I'm sitting there with a notepad writing it down. I don't want to forget it, but he'll [say,]

"No, no. Don't write down my secret recipe." So, I need to keep my written recipes locked away.

My favorite holiday is Thanksgiving because it's family time. Christmas [is the same]. I always liked the vibe of Christmas, but it was different because it was more external and materialistic [than Thanksgiving]. It was always cool because we didn't have to go to school. It did snow basically every winter in Connecticut. We always got to go sledding, but Thanksgiving was always special. My mom would get up early to start cooking. [She still does] to this day. She sent a group text on Thanksgiving [saying,] "Anybody who doesn't have anywhere to go on Thanksgiving can come [to our house]." [She] didn't want anyone eating alone on Thanksgiving. Thanksgiving was always special because everyone in my family was together.

[If I left,] I would like to come back to Hastings. I would love to be [in] an administrative role here at the college at some point, whether it be academic dean, dean of student engagement, academic affairs, or president of the college. Those aren't necessarily goals I have, but they are things I'm curious about. If I stay for two more years, I'll have been here for ten years. That's a decade of time spent here, of time building my legacy. If I leave Hastings, I would come back.

I was born in 1941 in Nebraska, close to the South Dakota line. I moved to Trumbull, Nebraska, roughly sometime when I was around two or three. Then I came to Hastings when I was four [and I] have been here ever since, except when I got married and left [to] Grand Island for a year. My mother grew up in Naples, Nebraska. I think my dad was from here too. His family had a big farm and ranch. They built the Navy depot here. It was pretty cool. The naval people were very nice, and we even had more marines stationed there. We had a barracks there, but all that's gone now.

I go to the Hastings Bible Church. I call myself a gypsy, because I go to different churches every now and then. But I've been with this Bible Church for a long time now. When I grew up I was in the Second Presbyterian Church. It was a couple blocks from our home, so that's where my family went. I went all through school in Hastings, and I graduated from Hastings Public School in 1959.

I worked out at the Regional Center when it was open for about a year. Then I met my husband [Frank]

june mueller

Interviewed by AJ Osborn

and married and that was the year we spent in Grand Island. We came back here [and] started raising a family. I did little odd jobs, [but] I wanted to be home to raise children. I started to work later, when they were older. I worked at Runza drive-in because they would work around my schedule, and I could be home with [my] children. After they graduated we opened up Frankfurters. It was a little shop where we sold hot dogs and nachos. It was [also] a game room and we had video games. It was in town on South St. Joseph Street. It was open probably four or five years. After that, I got into TCBY, The Country's Best Yogurt. My kids always worked for me in both places. Always. I figured I'd teach them some good work ethics

[I] met [my husband] in Grand Island when I was eighteen. He was the manager of the skating rink, and I went there to go skating. They had a couple of ladies' choices, so I thought, "Well, I'm gonna ask him." Then when we were ready to go home, he took my skates off, helped me get my shoes on, asked me my phone number, and asked if he could call me sometime.

[We have] three children. My oldest child is Doug Miller, and he lives in town. He's an electrician. My daughter is the middle child, and she lives in Independence, Missouri. She has three boys that all play baseball, so we go to a lot of baseball games. We've really enjoyed it.

My youngest son passed away. He died six months ago. [Interviewed November of 2018].

[My husband and I] used to square dance. We really enjoyed that. We did it as a couple. Now, I like to read on my own. I like to do Sudoku. I do yoga and I have done Tai Chi. Tai Chi is for balance really. I'm not an artsy person, even though my friends try to get me to do little projects. My hobbies are gardening, flower gardening and vegetable gardening. I prefer flower gardening. We grow a lot: zucchini, onions, and we used to grow corn, peas, and beans, really everything, even winter squash. [I still do it now] by the smaller scale.

We used to fish and hunt. Frank taught all the boys gun safety and how to handle a gun. Even when they were little, they could go out with him and walk fields for pheasants. They would have to carry a stick and had to pretend it was a real gun. He was really tough on them to make sure they were safe. That's about all we did, fishing, hunting, and camping. We've always celebrated Christmas as a family. We always did birthdays when the children were at home. We even extended that for a while. My sister's children got together for birthdays and always had family time. [We] love to play cards together. If you ever become part of this family, you have to play cards. We usually play pitch and we played a lot of board games. Every Christmas, when the kids were small, we [would] get a new board game. We spend New Years together. That's why [we] never went out. We figured we spent the year with our kids. We were going to see it out with them.

I hate to say it, but we don't have much opportunity here for young people really. They usually move away and get better jobs somewhere else. We're trying to change that, but I haven't seen the changes come about yet. Hastings is controlled by a few people who have kept businesses. We have a problem with that. That's why we haven't grown for a while. We have kept businesses from coming into town. When I have opened businesses here I've had to jump through hoops to get it open, because they want to keep the town as is. That's sad, because maybe with more places more people would come. [There would be] more opportunity for [young] people to stay after school. There's not a lot to do, so it can be very boring for people. They should make it easier for new businesses to come to town. That would be one of the things that would improve Hastings. We have a lot of food and restaurants, but we need something besides that.

This is my home. I like the seasons. I could never move somewhere [there] wasn't seasons. Hastings is pretty friendly. You walk down the streets [and] you can say hello or smile and wave to the stranger and they smile and say hello back. For the most part, the people in Hastings are pretty down to earth. I like the small-town atmosphere. We can get any place within five minutes. Hastings is a safe place. [When I was younger] you didn't lock your doors. We didn't have air conditioning for many years. When I was little we could we could sleep in our yard and not be afraid, so it was just, it was safe. It's a friendly community, and there are activities when you're older that you can get involved in to make acquaintances and friends.

tamisha osgood

Interviewed by Alex Hartwick

I am originally from Toronto, Canada. My background is Chinese culture from Guyana, South America. I've tried to do a lot of Caribbean and Canadian traditions here with my family like Thanksgiving is in October. It's usually around Columbus Day, which is a busy time. Food is a huge part of that. Good food I grew up with is completely different than American food. I try to incorporate that in to my children's lives and my husband and he's willing to eat anything. Music is also a part of my culture: Caribbean music, Soca, and Reggae. I grew up with that. I dreaded, bringing that to my children because they don't like it, but I try. We go back to Toronto every year. My traditions aren't tied to my religion. I just felt I had a good opinionated family, support, and love. So, a lot of what I do is just about that. The religion is separate from that. [My husband's] Christmas traditions are different from my family because his mom is really over the top—she loves Christmas.

I was kind of disconnected from the community of Hastings and American culture. I had American friends and so I've heard about things. I took part in American Thanksgiving several years being out here, but it was an adjustment to get used to Thanksgiving and Black Friday [because] we don't do that in Canada. [Our holidays] are done differently, so it's been an adjustment and I've been here for a long time. I graduated in 2006. I feel like I grew up differently. This might be a cultural difference. If you go into a home, take off your shoes and Americans don't do that. That's just one little thing! I think because I grew up with a Canadian/Caribbean background there's just a different respect to adults. I grew up [believing that having] respect for elders is a big deal. I grew up with the old-school approach I try to instill in my family and children, but I'm pretty laid back.

    I think my parents were very strict. I couldn't go very many places, like I couldn't go to parties. I couldn't do all these things. There were some school functions I could go to, but I would say [my parents were] definitely stricter. I had a little bit more expectations at home, like chores, and responsibility such as cleaning, cooking, and other stuff around the house. I grew up with my grandparents and my mom. So, there's just a little bit more of that old-school approach. I remember me and a friend of mine wanted to go out and my mom was like, "No." It didn't make any sense to try to rebel because it would totally backfire. Caribbean people don't rebel against their parents. Like, you just didn't do those things. However, in American culture, I feel like you see that [rebelliousness] a little bit more for whatever reason. It could be different parenting styles. You'll always hear that it's just a little stricter in the Caribbean family background, and it's not that we're out doing stuff but it's a tougher environment. I'm like this with my children now. My husband and I, we're on the same page with how we parent for the most part. There are differences because we grew up differently; my husband is an American.

It's not hard to assimilate my culture into American culture. I've adapted to being here, but I miss being around more diverse people. Within the comfort of my house, I partake in my traditions and stuff. I'm okay with that. I try to go home every year because that helps me to be comfortable here because I get to go home and interact with friends in the culture and eat good food. So, I mean that's just kind of that's how I balance it. Also, my husband is so supportive. He'll eat food from my culture, even though that's not something you'll find in his teeth. The last two summers, the kids got to participate in the Caribbean Toronto Carnival parade. It's a street festival. There are bands, Trinidadian paintings, dancing and parts of my culture. It's almost too much but I was like, they had to go and be the in the parade. This year we couldn't make it because we had a [schedule] conflict.

I didn't go to high school here so it's tough because I came here to go to college. I think it's very similar to my high school, which is pretty, pretty similar to Hastings. I think it's very comparable. The standards to get into university are a little different. That was different from what I hear of the kids in high school what they have to do. So that was kind of hard, especially being a foreigner coming to a country. That was a little tricky, but I made it work. I don't want to say Canadians put more value into education, but education is a different priority. That's the difference. They don't value the academics; sports are a high priority maybe some places higher. In Canada, I feel like sports are on the back burner. If you want to pursue any kind of sport, you're in a club and it just looks different than high school sports are here. That's a huge difference.

Here's the deal: I feel like I'm different than anybody. Black students can stick together and we're comfortable together, but I never felt truly comfortable because they weren't Caribbean. There were a few [students] that came from The Bahamas and I clicked really well with them. Black Americans are different than Caribbean people. We have different values and we grew up differently. So, I struggled but not really struggled. I came out here focused on track, school, and being a good person on the inside. I cared about friends but I just [knew] they weren't the people I felt I had to hang out with. Just because, we just saw things differently and we made moves differently. And so that's always been a struggle for Black Americans and Caribbean people. In Nebraska, like it's very rare to meet somebody who came from Caribbean background. Despite our differences, as a mom I want [my children] to know and understand African-American history.

The governments are run completely differently. Canada has universal health care, which I think is a huge deal. I always feel kind of disappointed and sad for people in America who obviously can't afford health care. [Therefore they] don't go for dentist checks every six months or even annually. They can't afford it. Those things make me sad because I think everybody has the right to medical care but that's not the case because not everybody can afford it. That's a huge difference that bums me out. The cost of insurance is ridiculous, and I know Canadians pay more taxes to pay for universal health care. There are a lot of flaws and everything isn't perfect. However, I have two babies, so to have a baby it's pretty much free, not really free, but I'm not paying $2,000 out of pocket like when Americans have babies. Insurance is only going to cover so much and, it's just too expensive, expensive. It adds up fast. So, I have friends who say, you [should] just come back home and have a baby.

The other [difference] for me as a mother is maternity leave. Just like in Europe, they give up to a year and maybe even more in maternity leave. Canada [originally] gave three to six months for mothers and fathers would have about half of that for paternity leave. Now, it's up to a year! I heard it might be about eighteen months and that's amazing! That's great [time] you are spending with your child. It's precious time. I wish America would get on board with that. I think it's necessary, but I don't know if we'll ever get there though. That's the sad part especially with the way the governing party believes in outdated social norms.

I miss the faster pace. Nothing takes longer than ten minutes in Hastings. However, driving to Lincoln is the longest road and it took me years to adjust to that. I try not to go very often but there's no place to get my hair done [in Hastings]. Actually, in my son's class there's probably like two or three, maybe five, kids that are black, which is huge. It's really nice especially here in this state. They go to Watson, which is a school on the north side of town. We wanted a small school and now it's blending.

My name is Melissa Pedroza. I am Hispanic. I was born in Grand Island, Nebraska. My mom was born in Texas. I never met my father, but apparently he was from Mexico. It was difficult [growing up in Grand Island] because we come from extreme, generational poverty. I lacked a lot of my basic needs like food, shelter, and feeling safe because of the environment that we lived in. [I lived there for] most of my life. That's where I grew up until I moved to Hastings.

I'm the school community liaison. I really appreciate my job. I'm also a provisional mental health practitioner. I work with kids who are at high risk. Coming from my background, I'm passionate about my job. We work with students who have behavioral issues. It can be difficult until you build that trust with them. I like to motivate them. I feel like a lot of our students lose hope and feel like they have no future ahead of them. I try to motivate them to let them know that their future can be so much different. I try to help them understand how education can open the doors for them to better their future. What I enjoy most about my job is

Interviewed by Jeremiah De Irish

melissa pedroza

instilling hope for a better future in students. At one point, I was one of those students who felt like my life couldn't be anything more. I needed just that one person to believe in me.

I met my husband and moved here to Hastings. [I enjoy] the atmosphere. I like raising my family here just because it's a smaller place. I went to Central Community College. When I started out, it felt like a family. It's a small college and small campus.

My mom was a migrant worker. They rolled beans milo, corn, picked the lemons, oranges, watermelon. Growing up we moved from place to place. We were in and out of different schools. That's one of the reasons education wasn't important to me. As I got older, my life had changed, and I had my children. I wasn't looking to be moving everywhere. I didn't want to disrupt their education.

[My family] came from extreme poverty. My mom had seven children. She was a single mother. When I would say, "Mom, look, that lady has a new car. I wish we had that." She always knocked it down. I don't think knowingly, but she'd be like," Oh, we can't have that. Because we don't have money." It was, "Don't even dream it or think it because you can't have it." It was a feeling to not even aspire to have more because this is our life, and this is what it will always be.

I was very close with my brother. We were always together. We were close in age. We could talk to each other about things. I am very close with my siblings. I'm the oldest.

I wouldn't say [my overall childhood experience] was the best. I can say that I lived in a loving home. I felt loved, but I lacked a lot of things. No kid should have to live that way, but a lot of kids do. It's really heartbreaking.

[In high school] I started working at Hunan's as a waitress. I dropped out of high school. So, I had to start from the bottom. I had to get my GED. [The process was] very difficult, because you had to pay for the test. I had been out of school for so long. I had missed out on all those years of education. It played a big factor. When I took the test, the only thing I didn't score well on was math.

I became a teenage parent. After having my children, I realized I [had to] do something different with my life. Then I started working in production jobs and had a taste of life. That's what started to change my mindset.

So, one of the things that really changed my mindset, [was when] my husband had an accident. He hit a deer and that scared me. He was the sole provider. If something were to happen to him, I'd have nothing.

I basically depended on him. I was a homemaker. That's really what caused me to say, "Oh, I need to do something with myself."

When I was working production jobs, my mother-in-law was the one taking care of our three children. All of a sudden, she got sick and died. My mother-in-law, she was a huge support for us. Losing her like that was very difficult. My husband had deep depression. He didn't want to come out of the room. It took a big toll on us. She was always there emotionally and just to hear us and to help us.

So, I didn't have a babysitter anymore. That's when I finally decided I needed to look into college and financial aid. I enrolled at CCC. My professor connected me with some resources on campus to guide me because I was really lost. I did come out on top. I passed all my classes. There were many times I wanted to throw in the towel, raising four kids, being a wife, and going to school full-time. I completed something, and it boosted my self esteem. I loved learning. I loved school.

I did [pursue my PhD], and I actually just graduated [last] December. My master's [is] in mental health counseling. So, for me and my family, I'm the first of my whole generation from way back God knows when they all started to ever have went to college. Number one to have even went and to have received a master's degree.

[Having a child at a young age] was a scary experience. The most important thing was [that] my husband stuck by me. We weren't married at the time, but he stood by me. That gave me some sense of relief. But it still was very difficult. I don't wish that upon anybody. It's not that you can't come out on top, you can, but it's just more difficult. You lose your childhood. I had to grow up faster than most people, but I was willing to do that for my kids. I wanted them to be my top priority.

Right now, I can honestly say [that] I don't regret anything that happened in my life. It's made me who I am. I'd hate to see somebody have to follow in my shoes, living the life that I did. I don't regret it. I think it's made me strong, but if I could start all over and say, "Oh, you're going to be born into a family with both parents. You're not gonna have to struggle that much. You're not gonna have to worry about going to bed without any food on the table or where you're going to live tomorrow"—that would be much better.

I have a son who's going to be graduating college in May. I got another son who already graduated high school. My daughter is a senior this year, and I have a junior. Everything that I've instilled in them about education. We stopped that generation of poverty, of not believing in education. I grew up instilling in them the importance of education, something that I wasn't taught. For them it wasn't *if* I'm going to go to college, it's I am going to go to college. My kids will tell you like, "My mom never let us miss school."

I don't look down upon people who don't have a college degree either. My husband doesn't have one. He's just more hands on hard worker. I always told my kids, "I really would love [for] you guys to have [a] college degree, but if you want to go work hard labor for the rest of your life, you can." Just know that when you get older, it's going to be much tougher for you. If you ever have the opportunity to move up in your position, and somebody has a degree and you don't, [they're] probably going to get that position. If they're trying and they're working, I feel like they're equal. At least they're trying. I valued education. I try to open that up to them. I think a lot of kids don't know that college is different [from high school]. The kids who have never been exposed to college have no clue. I try to help educate them on that level.

[What I enjoy most about my children is] who they become, seeing [the] sacrifices that I made. I made some good kids. I made kids who valued education, and that we were able to stop the generation of poverty. It didn't just happen like with me. I stopped it, but then my brothers and sisters saw me go to school, and my sister went to school. She has her family now and her kids. It's all about school. It was just that one person who believed in me and motivated me and was there for me, who helped change that. When they say that it only really takes one person, it honestly just takes one person to help somebody. If that person changes, that person can go on and help other people change.

[I'm most proud of myself because] I'm still standing. I'm still positive. I look at the positive things in life, because I feel like I lived so [many] negative things. It was always the negative. Even if something bad happens, I always try to find the optimistic [way to] look at the good things. I gotta find some value that's positive.

I wouldn't want my daughters or my kids to get married as young as I did, to start a family as young as I did. I want them to live their childhood and not struggle as much. I want them to start off with the right foot and not the left foot. [I want them to] have their education and their house so they don't have to be struggling. When they have kids, they're set. They're not always trying to dig themselves out.

[Success] has to do a lot with the way I grew up and not having things. Success is having food on my table, having a roof over my head, and a vehicle to drive. Material things come and go. I can find happiness in the smallest things. There [are] people where it doesn't matter how much money you have, or what [a] big house you live in, or the nicest car you can have. They still can't find happiness.

Someday, [I] hope to be a good grandma. I haven't really thought about it because I still have kids at home. I'm still working. I love education, but it's just a lot of work and expensive. I feel complete. I feel like I've been able to accomplish the goal that I have set for myself. I've overcome and achieved them way and beyond, the things that I thought were impossible. When I was growing up, I felt stupid and dumb. That's not something I'm embarrassed of. When I went to CCC, they do the compass test score on you. I probably started out so low at those scores. I had to start at the lowest levels. I started from scratch. I had to build from zero to build myself up. I took the time to learn it all again. I try. That's the most important thing is when people try. If you really want something, you can attain it. Is it going to be easy? No, it's gonna be a lot of hard work, but it's attainable. If you try hard, you can do it.

My marriage has grown. When I started going to school. it was a cultural change too. Usually, the woman stays home, she takes care of the kids. That's the kind of culture I grew up in. Not that everybody who's Hispanic or Mexican grows up that way, but in my situation, that's the way it had been when my mom was married. She's the one who stayed home, cooked, cleaned, maintained the house, [and] took care of the kids. I fell into the same role. That's what I was doing. So, I had to break down some of those cultural expectations in order to go to school, in order to have a job. It's a whole different culture. In my first professional job, I was a home visitor and I had to go do visits with men and everything else. It was a culture shock. We had to adjust to our whole lives, because my life had changed. It wasn't the same.

My husband was willing to make those changes and grow with me and support me. If he wouldn't have been, I wouldn't be sitting here today. There [were] times he had to take on the role of being mom and dad at the same time when I was in the room: studying for tests and reading online materials. Even up to this point, although the kids [are] older, but he [is] taking on those extra roles as well, so I can be able to continue on with my education.

Yes, I do [feel frowned upon for being a young parent]. Sometimes I've been at my daughter or son's functions and hear, "You're his mom? My gosh, I thought you were his sister." They'll say things like that or make comments. You just have to learn how to live with other people's opinions and not let them bug you. Look how far I've come. The most important thing is what you think about yourself.

Is it easy? Hell no, it's not easy. It's a lot of hard work. But look, your hard work pays off in the long run. It pays off. It might not feel like it is right now, but in the long run, it does pay off and I'm living proof of that. Sometimes, I'll share a little bit of my story with [my students or kids] to help them see. Don't judge a book by its cover because it's easy to think from just what you see on the outside, but you don't know the things that I lived through. I would motivate them to continue on because their hard work will pay off at the end.

I don't have a specific religion. I did get married Catholic because my husband was Catholic, but I grew up in a Pentecostal church. I feel like God is the same. I don't really care what church anybody goes to. If you believe in God, I feel like he's the same one. He hears you if you're praying to Him.

God was my number one that I call on for strength, wisdom, pacience, and guidance. There're times I'd be at my knees crying because it was a lot. I honestly feel like He helped me. I believe in God. He does help me every day, with my kids and different struggles in life. I've always depended on him.

We believed in Jesus growing up. My mom [taught] us to always pray and believe in God, that he would always be there for us. I grew up believing that. I honestly believe that I need God in my life in order to continue to survive in certain aspects [of] my life. I had to change because I was not perfect. I would ask for strength from him to help me change those things. I strongly believe that He helped me.

My name is Wayne Perez and I'm thirty-three years old. I live in Hastings, Nebraska.

I own a residential and commercial cleaning business here in town. I have two sons who are thirteen and ten years old. I moved to Hastings in 2014 and I moved here to be in a relationship.

I was born and raised in Ottumwa, Iowa on September, 1985. My family is originally from Ottumwa, Iowa. My mom and dad divorced when I was seven. I lived with my mom for ten years and saw my dad on the weekends here and there. And now there's no relationship with either my parents. We grew up in a variety of different churches. My mother was married to this man who wanted to go to all these different kinds of churches. We just went wherever he went. I mean, there was church there, but we weren't committed to it. Sometimes we go to this church and sometimes another church. Now, I don't attend church, but I have a personal relationship with God. Political[ly] right now everything's in turmoil, and so it's hard to share that. I'm more Democrat than Republican, and I try to

Interviewed by Josh Merithew

wayne perez

express my views whilst listening to both sides. I just try to stay neutral and don't discuss politics a lot, but I am a Democrat. I'm not involved in any political organizations.

I went to high school in Ottumwa. Then I went through community college two or three times. I went to the community college in Ottumwa and then the community college in Des Moines, Iowa. I decided college wasn't for me and I just took the career path. I was trying to major in business during my time in college. I guess it turned out because I now own a business. When I moved here, I wasn't sure what I wanted to do. I had many different jobs in my life. I thought, "What can I do with my experience?" but also be my own boss. I did not like working under people. It's just something I noticed about myself. I'm not a follower. I like to do my own thing, create my own things and be a leader. When I turned thirty, I worked for another cleaning company and I decided I don't really want to listen to other people. I want to have my own ideas. I took my business background, which was in HR payroll, I sold insurance for a while. Then I thought "I'm good at cleaning." All that kind of came together as, "Okay, I'm going to start my own business." I started cleaning houses. Now, I have seventeen employees and we have a great business in the community and can give back and it's great. I can be my own boss and school did help to a certain level, but I didn't need it to do what I'm doing.

I met my boyfriend in 2014 on social media. We're gay and we have kids; when someone sees that you kind of sticking out to somebody. He noticed that I had two sons and then just messaged me on Facebook one day and said "Hi." Then we had a few dates. Gus' personality and humor drew me to him. A lot of guys that haven't been in a relationship before that don't have children can have a hard time with someone like me who has kids and has financial obligations to them. You need to find a partner who can understand that and not think about that negatively. He has a daughter, so he understands, and it's nice to find that in somebody. I've always been kind of nervous about myself. I don't want to be around people that are exactly like me. I'm not talking about skin color or anything like that. I'm just saying I've always wanted to get out and explore other things and meet other people. Gus is different than me and I like that. I like to learn in my relationships, whether it's cultural or family things that they do, such as food and going places. That's wonderful to have in a relationship and it's just nice to have that difference. I'm able to learn and grow as a person myself from being with him.

[Gus interjects to tell a story about their relationship] Our relationship is unique in some ways. One day somebody on Instagram followed us, and they made a report of our relationship: having kids, being married, being Mexican and American, this whole thing together. We didn't know about it until somebody called us and said, "Hey, have you seen the report that's going around on social media? It has 3,000 shares." We are like, "What are you talking about? Wow." Lifetime channel contacted us because we're trying to get married this year on September twenty-ninth. Lifetime said, "Hey, would you guys be interested in having your wedding on live TV? We will pay for everything. The only thing you have to change is the wedding day. You will have to have an interview with a casting producer with a producer." We went through all the steps but unfortunately, we didn't get picked and we cancelled the wedding. I mean something interesting and different.

[Wayne] In my spare time I hang out with my boyfriend a lot. I call him Gus, but his name is Carlos and we've been together for almost five years. He has a daughter and I have two sons from previous marriages, we just hang out with them and spend time with family. We go to the YMCA a lot. I exercise five, six days a week, so busy. I'm interested in a lot of health and fitness. Making sure I eat right, take care of myself, doing things with my children. We like to travel so we go to Mexico every year to visit his [Gus] family who lives there. Gus got a lot more interesting story than me. We visit them a lot. I've been able to see different parts of the world. I love traveling and I plan to continue to do that. I like to go outside in the parks, walk around. I'm boring. We like to go to Kool-Aid Days which is every year, which is kind of a Hastings thing. We like to just make sure that we're always trying to go out with our friends [especially] if they're inviting us to something or some event in the community. We try to attend different things.

I have a thirteen-year-old son named Lucas and a ten-year-old son named Logan. And they're from a prior marriage to my ex-wife. We were together for ten years, we dated in high school, and I thought I was doing the right thing. We decided to have children and they're so open to me and to Gus. They're just a wonderful part of our life. I don't know what life would be like without them. It's just great to be a parent and that's another blessing in this world. Typically, I see my kids about once a month and then the summertime because they're out of state. We're with Ava every other Friday and every other weekend. We take her to Girl Scouts, swim meets, piano lessons, Adventure Land, or sometimes we go to birthday parties. We try to stay busy every time we go out together. We try to make sure that she's out with us socially, so that people can see us as a family as well. When my children are here, we're all together and it's hectic, people fight and argue but we make it work. It's a blended family. There's tension in the girls versus boys. We just do a lot of family activities with them.

Since we're not a traditional family we don't really follow the social norms; we make our own [traditions] up as we go. Every summer we take a family trip to go to Iowa and go to Adventure Land. Every year we take a trip to Mexico. On holidays our kids usually spend time with their moms and then we do our own thing. We think they should be with their mothers because they've got new families on that side with other things going on. Normally we just try to make up our own as we go, and we've figured it out along the last four or five years. It's tricky. We don't follow any tradition. We follow our own, we do our own thing. Like we are the new normal. From his [Gus] Mexican culture to my American culture, where they're different holidays and different things to celebrate. There are some other traditions that might blend together. We [Americans] celebrate Halloween and they [Mexicans] celebrate Day of the Dead, so we just try to combine them together. One year we dressed up as Day of the Dead. I don't know; we just figure it out.

Some of the most important things that I want to teach my children is that they should always take care of themselves first and worry about their health [meaning] taking care of their mind and their bodies. I want them to be aware that not everybody else is going to take care of them the way that they can take care of themselves. They've always got to make sure that they do that and not always worry about what other people are doing, thinking, and saying. Example: if someone is bullying them, I want them to be secure enough in themselves to be like, "You know what, whatever." Having a gay father and a gay step dad is kind of a mental struggle for them and I know that. I'll frequently ask them, "Are you okay with things? How do you feel about this?" That other value is just making sure that they accept people no matter who they are, even if they're different than you. You don't always have to understand why they are how they are. You don't have to understand or know everything about somebody to care about them or show them respect. I just want to make sure that they know to take care of themselves, have respect for other people, and be kind most of the time. Just be a nice person and don't judge. Everybody has that innate thing where we judge immediately and then we have to kind of reel it in. I try to teach them to think before they speak. Even with Ava, she's more American than Mexican culture. [We teach her] this is the language that we speak as a family and this is this is what we'd like for you to continue that. You are still Mexican American, just making sure that she was aware of that too. Just be open minded. In Hastings especially everybody thinks Mom, Dad, and kids, and that's the family. That's *a* family. A family can be anything you want it to be. Those are some of the values that I feel we put into our household.

Hastings is very small. There's not a whole lot to do, but the things there are here to do are pretty fun. It is mostly white people. There's not a lot of cultural differences, but you can find little areas in the community that there are [diverse]. Once you become part of that, you see that. Example, Gus is a Mexican and I'm not. If I didn't know him, I probably would have had no idea about the Mexican culture that's here in Hastings. There's quite a bit. There're places to eat that are Mexican. There are different traditional things that they bring in like at Kool-Aid Days. It's not all whitewashed but at first glance that's how it appears. I come from a bigger city where there are trans, black, gay, straight, lesbian people. In Hastings, it's very hard to find that community; we feel a little solo out here. There're not very many gay people in the community that are really outspoken. There's another business owner in town that's [a part of the community]. A couple of them that are gay. Another way I would explain Hastings is that a lot of the people here are kind even if they're not, as I described, "different." Most people are very kind to us and very welcoming. I would tell them [an outsider] that we may not be as culturally diverse as other places, but there are a lot of kind people here. You can find them. Social media helps because we can find different groups on there and know who we can be around.

I do like Hastings. The reason I like Hastings is it's safe. There's not a lot of crime here. There is a lot of opportunity here too for our business and for even future businesses. Being in this business has taught me that there's a demand for other areas of work. I like Hastings because there's room for growth. I would say one of best things about Hastings is that it's a small town, but it has a lot of open-minded people. That's why we have stayed here. Why I stayed here. Another great thing is that it's safe for kids and the schools are great. The teachers here do a wonderful job. We know a lot of them through the YMCA and they're so kind. I think that the one thing that I'd say is that there's room for growth and that they should allow more growth in Hastings, if I had to pick something negative. Another good thing about Hastings: I used to work for Hastings College in their food service department. I did their payroll there in their office. I would say that Hastings College is great for Hastings too. It's probably one of the best things. To have such a great school with the staff there. The professors are very knowledgeable and educated people. They bring a lot to this community and what they do. We also have the community college; so, there's a couple of choices in this town.

I would say the best thing about Nebraska is the Huskers, but they haven't been doing too well this year and I don't watch football. Nebraska is great, because again, it's a smaller populated state. There's not as much crime here. There's a lot of jobs here. I feel like there's not a lot of unemployed people here. I think with the reports that came out, the numbers look great. I have a business mind so I kind of think like that. Plus, you have options close to Hastings, such as Lincoln or Omaha, where you can immerse yourself with different people and get out of Hastings for a while. A break. A breather.

One thing I don't like about Nebraska is the death penalty that they just put back into effect. We had to revote on that, I think, last year. I don't think it's going to deter any crime. That's an argument we can have later. Another thing about Nebraska is that people like us who want to vote for different candidates on different ends of the spectrum for political reasons, we just feel, like, defeated because no matter what Nebraska is a Republican state and always will be. We manage, and we get through it.

We've experienced a couple of incidents of discrimination. There's outright discrimination where it's just plain to see and then there's other discrimination where it's more passive aggressive. I experience discrimination mostly because I'm gay. Gus, he might have a different reason because people are racist in the community. I've heard people make jokes about Mexicans or Spanish people. We were at Mary Lanning and we were sitting in the waiting room. This guy walked in to be seen and I don't know what set him off, but something set him off. He started cursing and screaming at me, "You f—king gay." I kind of blew it off but at the same time, you must watch out because people are violent. The security came, got him, and took him out. Of course, they apologized and everything else. It's not your fault. People are just jerks. People are just a—holes to be honest.

The other incident was when we were planning for the wedding. Everybody kept telling us, "Oh, contact this guy for catering. He's the best." We saw that it's one of the top ten best caterers in Nebraska. We decided to contact him. I emailed him and said, "Hey, this is a wedding date. Do you have anything open?" He said, "Sure. Come down, meet with me." He didn't know that I was gay. I didn't explain that in the email. I just said I was having a wedding. We get there and as soon as we got there Gus told me, "This is a no." I was like, "How do you know?" and he was like, "Just wait." The conversation should've been longer than five minutes but that's all it was. He was like, "Oh, well I'll have to check. I don't think we can do it now." I just felt like that was passive aggressive, where people aren't necessarily outright about it by saying,

"Oh, I'm not going to serve your wedding because you're gay." You told us [the date] was empty and then you're like, "No, sorry." He said, "Oh, I'll get back to you if it's open," and he never got back to us. A week later, we contacted him and asked, "Hey, so what's going on?" He replied, "Oh, no, I can't do it. I'm sorry." It was bad. I never want to paint a light that he seems hateful and discriminatory because I must be careful as a business owner what I say. It could affect my income and my employees. Things have happened, but most of the things that have happened have always been positive. People know us as a unit. They're like, it's Gus and Wayne. Wayne and Gus. We have each other and that helps.

One way for Hastings to become a better community is for more people in the community to step out of their comfort zone. They should do things that they necessarily wouldn't do in their everyday life. Every day people complain on social media about things whether it's racial inequality, LGBTQ+ rights, and different social issues. However, in the actual community they do nothing to help the situation. Unlike me, they're not going out and putting themselves into a relationship where they're dating someone of a different culture or a different race and being accepting of that. They're just kind of standing behind the scenes and complaining and not getting out on the dance floor doing something about it. People need to invite their neighbors over who are different than them, to sit down and talk to them. I don't remember the last time a straight guy ever walked in and said, "Can I talk to you?" People aren't getting out there and talking to each other. They're relying on technology and staying in their own groups and doing their own thing. I must put myself out there. Gus had to put himself out there. Gus is one of the very few Mexican people in this community that are involved with white people. A lot of times people just stay in their own language and their own corners and I just wish that that would change. Not in just Hastings, but everywhere. Just get out of your comfort zone. Always say hi to somebody you don't know

sam and elizabeth (ella) rathod

Interviewed by Elizabeth Hansen

I [Sam Rathod] was born in 1945, in the city of Jabalpur, India, where my parents were students at The Methodist Seminary. I grew up in a Parsonage. After graduating from the seminary, my dad was assigned to a church in a small village. Along with my family, there were only few more Christians in the village. When I was six years old, my parents sent me away to a Methodist boarding school. The reason my dad wanted me to go to the boarding school was we were a minority and most people were Hindus, and they looked down upon us. My dad was concerned that I will be discriminated against for being a Christian. I only went to the boarding school for a year. After serving a few other churches, my dad was assigned to the city where my wife Ella's family were members of our church.

In India, religion is important to everyone, regardless of what faith they follow or God they worship. In India 80% of people are Hindus, and Christians are only 3%, [which] accounts for Catholics, Protestants, and everyone else. In India we grew up as a religious minority. We respect and tolerate each other's faith and at times take part in each other's religious festivals. We don't have any problem wishing somebody Happy Diwali or a Merry Christmas or Eid Mubarak. Diversity is a daily way of life. India has a dark history of caste system and the lowest caste were untouchables. Under the leadership of Mahatma Gandhi, things began to change. Although Christians are only 3% in India, Christianity had a major role in influencing changing the class system, changing role and status of women through education, building boarding schools, colleges, technical schools, and hospitals. Christianity has taught me to be less prejudice and nonjudgmental towards other people. I am indeed proud to be a Christian

Later my dad came for further studies to United States at Asbury Theological Seminary in Wilmore, Kentucky. He also did his master's at Princeton. He returned to India but visited United States several times during his lifetime. Not only us, but his whole congregation was always eager to hear his fascinating stories about United States. After hearing his stories, we were all eager to come to United States. It was almost like going to heaven. I came to the United States in 1970 as a student. We [my fiancé and I] had to go to Mumbai to catch an international flight to come to the United States. Our families were all excited. We had a big farewell party. People came to see me off at our hometown's railway station with garlands and gifts. It was my first experience in the plane.

I had arrived at the height of Vietnam war, hippie movement, and unrest on college campuses. I attended Wheaton Graduate School in Wheaton, Illinois and majored in New Testament. After graduating at Wheaton, I went to a seminary on the west coast and earned my Doctor of Ministry in counseling. My first impression of the United States was that it was less crowded. In India, nearly a billion population, you look outside the window, all you see is people. Even now, I don't see people on the road whilst India is getting more crowded that you can't even walk on the street. Other things I observed is cleanliness, named streets, roads and houses marked with numbers. Also, the fast food restaurants were new to me as in India we only had street vendors.

We came to Nebraska in 1973, to serve our first church at Newman Grove, Nebraska, a town of 1,000 people. It was quite an adjustment as I came from a big city of two million people. We have lived in Hastings for twenty-one years. September fourth was our forty-seventh wedding anniversary. We were engaged in India and got married in Tulsa, Oklahoma. We have three children and three grandchildren. We had decided to assimilate in the American culture. One of the things we did to assimilate is give our children common American names like Nicholas, Janet, and Jason. I think we are treated good because of our public service profession. As years went by, we became part of the American culture. We are part of the Hastings community.

When we first arrived at Hastings First United Methodist Church, the congregation was not sure what an ethnic minority from India would do. The church never had a minority pastor before us. The congregation was mostly white, middle class, and educated. We also had lots of older people. There was apprehension among the church members whether they will understand my accent or whether we will understand the American culture. Once they got to know us, they accepted us wholeheartedly. We retired here, and we are part of the First United Methodist congregation. Even after retirement, I get lot of requests to do weddings and funerals by family members. Throughout the years, we have experienced their love and kindness in many forms. I am grateful to be a citizen of the United States and grateful to be living in Nebraska.

[Ella} My name is Ella Rathod. I was born in 1949 in India, north of Mumbai, in a state called Gujarat and I speak Gujarati. My dad was a physician and my mom was a nurse. When I was growing up in India, either you were rich or poor and there were very few middle-class people, but we were one of the few families who were middle class. My dad sent us to a school where the medium of instruction was English. I spoke British English from a very early age. Therefore, when I came to America, I had to learn American English.

I left India in 1971, after graduating from college to join my fiancé Sam at Wheaton college in Wheaton, Illinois. Both Sam and I came on a student visa. We were members of the same Methodist church in India where his dad was a pastor. At the time, people weren't traveling overseas as much. It was quite an experience. My family was very happy for me. According to the Indian tradition, they put flower garlands on us to send us off. The United States is an exciting destination for the people of India, especially to study in the United States. The big planes were very rare. I traveled on one of the very first 747 plane. I had never seen such a huge plane before.

We were not allowed to bring much cash from India, only $8.00. We were recipient of scholarships and grants to attend Wheaton College, and a couple of our friends helped us out in the beginning. I worked on the campus library and post office part time. The student visa prohibited us to work outside of the campus. I studied Christian Education at Wheaton College. I am grateful for Christianity and my culture. Christianity has many teachings on how to live, and both my culture and religion include kindness, goodness, and happiness. After our three children were born, I stayed home for few years, and I went into the library profession after they started school. I worked at Grand Island Public Library. Later I worked at the Mary Lanning Hospital Library.

We were in Chicago the first couple of years and in L.A. couple of years after. Coming from an Indian metropolitan city to Nebraska was quite different. It was roomier, less people, but it was nice. We were young and adventurous. In the beginning, we did feel a little out of place. Some people had a hard time understanding our accent and we had British English vocabulary. In the 1970s, Sesame Street was new on TV, and I enjoyed watching Sesame Street, just to learn the lingo. Just a few examples, what I call British English and American English ... you call it a sidewalk here, we call it footpath. If you're standing in line people will say, "You're standing in line." We will say, "we are standing in a queue." Those are the simple things, but little by little we got into mainstream.

We wanted our children to learn about Indian culture. Our Indian community was very small. We did things that were Indian at home, like the Indian dancing, Indian music, and Indian food. Our children loved it. When they grew up they learned to appreciate Indian culture more. We also wanted them to be comfortable in both cultures. We made sure that they didn't feel out of place at school. We also did everything in

American mainstream life. To this day, they are comfortable in both cultures.

What impressed me first of America was the roads and the layout of towns and cities. People were also very kind and helpful to me. That first impression has stayed with me. The biggest difference was food. We make curry, rice and flatbread. Indian food is very flavorful. In the 1970s there wasn't too much Mexican food; even pizza was rare. The food seemed so bland. I used to carry a small bottle of hot sauce in my purse all the time.

There is not too much of a difference in the United States from one state to another. In India every state has different food, different language, and different way of dressing. We grew up in the era of diversity. I noticed that some people here did not like signs posted in Spanish, while India has eighteen official languages. You go from one state to another state and it's another language. The morning news on TV are in eighteen languages. However, English is widely spoken. Hindi is our main language, along with the state language. Comparatively people are more reserved in America. In India, people talk to strangers with ease. When we travel by train, we always discuss politics. Not everyone agrees with each other, yet it is an open topic to talk about. This was the biggest change for me not to say a thing about politics or religion.

Sometimes American perception of Indian culture is very different. They just assume everyone in India is dirt poor and everybody is included in the caste system. But because of mobilization and education, the caste system is fading. India has a rich history and very rich culture. Indian culture is very hospitable. We have never seen out right racism, towards us. There are certain things that I look back on, I think "Oh, my goodness, that was prejudice, or that was racist." We have taught our children to go the extra mile in their jobs to prove their worth. Often, we have seen a new person walk in and is promoted before you. Sometimes, I see prejudice against minorities who are poor. It's not very outward, but if you look deep, it's there.

Hastings is a small, quaint town and people in Hastings are nice, helpful and friendly. Living in Nebraska, Sam has served predominantly white churches, but we have always felt at ease among the congregation, no matter where we went. The churches were always in forefront in welcoming the minorities and poor. I am grateful that I live in the greatest country, USA. Also, proud to be a Christian and United Methodist.

My name is Ellis Riley. I was born in 1992. I was born and raised in the north of England. On my mom's side, her parents were both born in Wales. I have quite a lot of Welsh in me. My mom was born in Wales, but moved to England very young, I believe before she was about six months old. There's a lot of Scottish on my dad's side of the family. His grandparents were born in Scotland, but his parents were born in England. I'm about five hours north of London, and grew up playing soccer, biggest passion also enjoyed playing rugby and skiing. Soccer is what brought me to the US essentially. In terms of faith in my family, [it] comes strongly from my mom's side. My grandma especially, is very big in her faith. She includes faith in everything she does; she's made it part of our daily life. I got a lot of my faith education through my grandma. My grandma influenced the fact that I went to faith-based schools because she pushed it on my mom and my dad like that. There's a fair amount of faith in our family, we're Christians, you know, generally Church of

Interviewed by Jenny Sells

ellis riley

England, because that's, that's kind of our local church, where we're from.

I kind of went a bit of everywhere to be honest in terms of my religious side and schooling. Our schooling is obviously different, like our elementary school we call reception. All our year groups are a little different to yours. I'll just try and make it simple. When I was in middle school, I was at the Church of England school. Middle school is between ages eight through twelve. At the age of twelve I entered high school and switched to a Catholic school. We're at high school from twelve to eighteen, essentially. My family didn't want me to go to a bad school with a bad reputation. We ended up applying to go to the Catholic school that was about fifteen minutes away. Thankfully, I got accepted because they only accepted a limited amount of non-Catholic students every year. It was a better environment for me. Thankfully, four or five of my close friends were also able to get into the Catholic school.

I am the most nonpolitical person. It's hard for me, because I moved out to the states when I was nineteen, which generally in England, like, you're not really worried about politics until you get into your twenties because it doesn't really affect you, or it doesn't affect you in the in the short term. And generally, our lives are so busy, that people aren't looking at the political side of things with a long-term vision more in England. I noticed that the norm in terms of politics was if it's not going to affect me in the next five years, I'm not really bothered about it. That's my point I was getting that is it's been tricky for me because I moved here when I was nineteen. I kind of have lost touch now with the UK side. Obviously, there's Brexit and stuff that's going on, if you're familiar with that. But even still with me, it looks like I'm going to stay in the States. It's not really going to affect me. I'm not too political. I don't really know enough either side and I honestly don't pay that much attention to either side. Now, I obviously pay attention to the immigration system being England and America, because I must know obviously, I'm on visas here. I must know which paperwork I have to have signed to be able to fly back and forth in and out of the country when I do go home to visit family. So, I'm aware of that side of things. But in terms of the parties and the election, I don't take too much interest in that.

The reason I chose to leave simply was I wanted to keep playing soccer full time. Basically, I knew I was going to go to college, and I'd already applied in England and I'd been accepted to the ones I wanted to go to. But you can't play soccer in England at college level in a serious way. It is known as a pub league because a lot of guys in the teams will have loads of drinks the night before a game, even more drinks after the game. There's no real coach involved but they'll train two or three days a week; it's mostly just the player's training each other. There's no leagues and conferences that you play. It's very unprofessional. That's why there's so many Brits out here who participate in college scholarship system in the university system here [in the States], because there's a lot of guys who want to play five, six, seven days a week taking care of their bodies in a professional environment with great facilities. And that's why I did it. I heard of it through a friend, a family friend, whose son had come out to play in the states a few years before. I went for a tryout with a company who would promote me to colleges to come out to America. Thankfully, I was good enough. I got brought on by the agency and they promoted me to schools. The agency tried to get me the best scholarship possible and the right fit for me as a school. That was my only reason to leave. Obviously, I like to travel. I'm an only child, so I've always kind of just like to go off and do things independently. Once I made my mind up I wanted to come to America, I was pretty much dead set on it. I didn't really have too many second thoughts once the process started, especially when I started speaking to colleges and coaches. It was really exciting for me, I love that process. My mom and dad were supportive. In reality, I love England for what it is. It's different to the United States in many ways. The reason for me leaving was not for anything negative. It was just for the want to do what I love to do which was soccer at the time.

Mum and Dad were obviously very sad, I think because I was an only child. It was just us three: me, my mom, and dad. I think made it a lot quieter when I left. The plus side they've been able to come visit America quite a lot. Now, it's we'll go see Ellis, so that's good for me, and I think they like it too. Now, they haven't visited Hastings too much. But when I lived in Florida, I think they came over three times in a year. I think it's been fun for them because they've been able to come and visit and explore America a little more. When I graduated in North Dakota, they managed to come over and we did a road trip down to Mount Rushmore, South Dakota, and through a few state parks and things like that. They've done things that I don't think they would have ever done if I hadn't had moved. I know they appreciate that for sure.

When I first came to the US, I did three semesters in North Carolina. Then I transferred to Jamestown, North Dakota. After I graduated there, I spent a year coaching in Florida on a work visa that you're entitled to after you graduate, you get one-year work visa to kind of, it's your chance to go somewhere and basically put your degree to use. I had a minor in coaching. I wanted to coach soccer, and I got offered a full-time position in Florida. Once that expired, I realized I wanted to be a GA at college. I'm the Grad Assistant at Hastings College for the women's soccer team. I also run a social media business for soccer coaches on the side. And I also thought, great, now I can get my master's degree. So, that brought me to Hastings. Now, Hastings, I would say seven years I've been here.

My first impression really was North Carolina. When I landed in Charlotte, North Carolina, I didn't know who I was looking for to pick me up. I just knew that the coach at my school was sending a player to come pick me up, but I didn't know the player. I felt fine all the way over because it was obviously very exciting. I was nervous and anxious, but excited. When I got to Charlotte I couldn't see who was picking me up and I was kind of stuck around there for about thirty minutes. People got their bags and left, and I stood there, like looking for someone; that one part for me was a bit like, oh my gosh. It would be nice if somebody showed up now, because, it's been a long day of traveling. I just left all my family behind for the next eight months, at least, it'd be nice to have a familiar face here right now. Thankfully, they showed up and I noticed their hat had the school logo on. I walked over, and I said "Hey, are you looking for me?" And it turned out to be the right guy. So, once I got picked up and brought to my school at the campus, it was beautiful. I was about forty minutes outside of Charlotte, at a Division 2 school about 3,000 students. Small campus but it was pretty. It was beautiful, very green and not too far from the ocean. Especially where Charlotte is, it's only like two hours or so away. And just there was a lot to do. I really liked it. That was a really cool place for me and I've always loved going back. I've always said I could always go back and live there because it was great. And I really liked it there. You've got a little bit of everything. The people are nice. That was a big first impression. I know it's a part of the Bible Belt area. People are so friendly. That also helped me settle in. I picked a great state to go to for me because I needed people who are going to be nice and friendly and made me feel comfortable. My first impression was great. I loved it.

We don't do Thanksgiving at home. I spent my first Thanksgiving with my roommate's family in South Carolina. The whole Black Friday shopping, which I'd never experienced before. At 1:30 in the morning, my roommate's mom and his sister banged on our door like, "Wake up we're going to shop." It was cool because I've never done it before. Now I think it's crazy. All that stuff was quite overwhelming. So that shows how my perception of America changed. The first year I was so excited to come home with about $200 worth of deals. Now, I would never go on Black Friday night because it's just crazy. It took me a while to get used to the little subtle things about the American way of life. Just like the lingo. People would walk past me, be like, "What's up?", and I didn't know what it meant at first for like the first month. Every time this one guy, I'd walk past would say "What's up?" and my response every day was, "Not much, like, I'm fine." In England, "What's up?" means "What's wrong?" And I would always be like, "Yeah, I'm fine with you." That was funny; I always laugh about that, because it's so true. This guy must have asked me what's up maybe ten times. And my response was the same every day until somebody finally told me because I asked somebody else. That was all part of me moving to a new country.

My perception [of America] has changed a lot since I moved here just because I lived in so many different places. Charlotte, North Carolina was more normal for me because we'd been to like Orlando, Las Vegas and New York [on] family vacations. At least I think I'd been to America on vacation maybe four [or] five times before I moved here. I at least had a sense of what I was coming to. Everything I'd seen before I came over was a lot of Division 1 soccer because that's what they present to you. That company that helps you get out here they present the UCLA's [and] Stanford's [but] reality is barely anybody goes to those schools. A lot of them are made up of American players, not international. It was really good my first year and then I kind of got a bit more of a welcome to reality when I got to North Dakota, but I'm glad I had the experience of my first year in North Carolina because that was what I was hoping it was going to be when I arrived, so I got to experience it. And then I also got to appreciate the other side.

The college system in North Carolina it was what I was hoping it was going to be. We had a great facility, like amazing facility for the Division 2, one of the best, the stadium was great, the grass was great, the equipment was great, everything was cool. You know, you got your own locker with your name on; you could, like, sit in your locker and it had your own little dim the lights inside; they would do all your laundry for you. They wash your boots, your cleats for you and stuff. Cool. That was like I felt like I was in a professional environment. And that was awesome. Then North Dakota, the people were amazing too, definitely didn't necessarily love living there. It's cold, small town, you get used to it and you start to appreciate it more. By no means would I say that it's a place where I could live forever. I'm a city guy. So, for me, it was very far away from what I'm used to. I am city guy, but I also love nature. There's also not much nature; that's very barren. So thankfully, there was a lot of other British people on the team. That helped me settle in, there was about twelve of us from the UK. The people were great, and the campus environment was good. The university was great. I just wish it was in a different location.

Well, essentially, my parents were having some financial issues. My mom was a little sick, so she couldn't work for a while. My dad was covering all the costs. The school I was at was a little too expensive, and I needed more scholarship that he couldn't give me to be able to stay. I was happy there. Then it was a case of because I was a Division 2 player, I also didn't want to stay in college for five years and redshirt. So, my options were go NAIA, because that's your best chance of not red shirting a year. I emailed every single school in the NAIA, and, looking back, it was one of those times where I had done my research. I knew which schools weren't very good [and] which schools that even if I got an offer, I was probably still want to say no to. I emailed every school because we were doing it for finances. If the school came to me with, say, a full ride, but the team was only okay. I would probably, obviously, still take an offer. It was a full ride. My ambitions for soccer are still quite high and the same degree or similar degree I needed to have available to me and I transferred. It was funny though, I committed to a school in Florida in West Palm Beach [however] I ended up in North Dakota. The coach in North Dakota at Jamestown, he would not stop calling me on the phone. He called me like four times in one week. I'd already verbally committed to the school in Florida. I'd signed my roommate and housing documents for the next semester already. I was waiting to figure out who I was going to be rooming with and we're signing off like deposits for housing and stuff like that. Anyway, he kept calling me and I got good vibes off the coach at Jamestown. He really wanted me to come. As much as I didn't want to go to North Dakota, he was almost convincing. He was the one who convinced me to go in the end, wasn't the area, it was him. We had the first phone call and he made me an offer. Then four days later, or the fourth phone call later after I'd already told him I'd committed to Florida, I was pretty sure I was going to Florida, he came back with a better offer. It was financially a pretty good deal for us; so, I called my parents again. I said look, I'm getting a good feeling from this guy. He really wants me to come here. So, I ended up going [to] Jamestown and backing out on the Florida option, which I can't say I regret it because I had a great [experience], especially my first season at Jamestown. If most people are given the chance they [would] choose Florida. There's always a hint of me that wonders what it would have been like spending two and a half [to] three years in Florida instead. Going to North Dakota was a lot different [because] it was a lot more of a blue-collar team. It taught me to appreciate the simple things. I remember we played on a grass field and the grass was like three inches long. It's all brand new and we didn't have a locker room, we had to walk five minutes to the field from inside the small center. We didn't have a scoreboard, we had to bring out a small clock and they plugged it into the main [circuit] to a bunch of wires; it was old school. I remember my senior year, we got a brand-new scoreboard built into the field and we appreciated it like crazy.

I would describe Hastings as a smaller Midwestern town with nice people and a friendly atmosphere. There's just enough to keep you occupied and busy. There're some nice touches to the area, like downtown is pretty, nice, neat, and [has] some cool places to eat. I'd say it's probably limited on things you can do outside of work environments. There's not too much you can go and do on a weeknight. There's one movie theater that's small and the bowling alley—I've never been to that, to be honest. In the summer, there's more stuff to do because the water park opens and a couple other things. Between October and March, the activities are limited by the weather conditions. I would tell people if you're going to Hastings, it's best to go between April and August, [you'll] at least be able to do the outdoor and the indoor things that you may want to do. Otherwise there's maybe not too much to do. Obviously, I'm here for my master's degree and coaching, which is what I enjoy and love to do. That's the most important thing for me being here. Alongside that, I've had no problems living in Hastings and I've enjoyed my time here so far.

I don't have any ideas on how to improve Hastings. I have not seen enough negatives to say anything against it. I think it's a pretty good and safe community here. As far as I'm aware, I may be wrong, but I have not heard things. My perception is that it's a simplistic but pretty safe place to be. I don't think there's too much to change.

I am twenty-six years old. I have four children and I have been married to my husband for three years. We just found out recently we are expecting our fifth, due March 15th, 2019. It's been exciting and crazy. I was born in Baltimore, Maryland, at John Hopkins Hospital on December 21st, 1991. I lived in Maryland 'til I was about ten. Then [I] moved to Brookville, Pennsylvania. I graduated from Brooksville High School, met my previous husband, and had my first child.

The East Coast is completely different than Nebraska. I miss certain things back there, like how you could just go down to the harbor and walk around and there was just so much to do down there than what there is here. It's more kid friendly here than what it was in Maryland.

My mother is from Maryland and my father was from Pittsburgh, Pennsylvania. My mom and dad got a divorce when we were young. My dad was in the military so my family's a big military family. He was Army National Guard.

sabrina rodriguez

Interviewed by Andie Paschal

[After high school] my mom was in Florida. I moved to Florida with my mother and I was living there. We went to Sea World. It was time for me to wind down because of everything I went through with bullying in high school. It was time for me just to find who I was again.

I am a Christian. I was baptized as [a] Christian. I went to church since I was a little kid. I quit going to church when I lived in Florida with my mother because I couldn't find a church I liked. So, when I moved up here, I started going to North Shore. I really like North Shore, so I'm getting back to going to church every Sunday. I haven't missed church since we moved here.

It was my grandfather and mom who took us to church every Sunday. We went to Bible school. We did a lot of stuff. My grandfather, he used to read out of the Bible to us as kids. It's just something that I grew up with and am passing down to my children. [I grew up] Catholic. I went to Catholic Church, but then I told my grandfather I didn't like it, so we tried a Christian church. That's where we started going every Sunday. It was the church that my mom went to as a child.

[The Catholic Church] just didn't feel right. You always get that feeling. When I step foot in a church, if I don't feel comfortable and I don't feel like it's where I'm supposed to be, I don't go back to it. When I set foot in North Shore, I knew that's where I was supposed to be.

They're saying at North Shore is, "You can come as you are, you are not judged here, we are all God's people." That's what I've been going with. That's the saying that I keep in my head every day now. [I've been going there] for about two months now. The kids love it.

They have kids' connection, which is for the kids. They go to one room for the babies and kids that are two and [younger]. They have a nursery for them. They do little activities about God with them too, so it's really nice.

[Politically,] I'm not registered. Why vote for something if you're not really gonna follow it? It is [a heated political climate right now]. Everyone says, "Trump just needs to get out of the office because he's not a good president." Why are we bringing this up? All it's going to do is start a fight. When people bring it up, I'm gone, bye.

I do not [work anywhere in Hastings]. I was living in Red Cloud, Nebraska. We came to Hastings to get out of that small town. The schools in Red Cloud weren't fit for kids with special needs, [such as] learning disabilities. I looked up some schools and asked a bunch of questions and Watson was the number one that met all of the kids' needs. That is where they're going.

We had family that lived here in Nebraska. We moved down here, and at that point in time, I was with my fiancé, which is my ex-husband now. I found out I was pregnant, and it was not a good relationship. After him and I split up, I moved back. I got stuff taken care of with my daughter, who is now six. I got a job at a nursing home in Red Cloud and I haven't left Nebraska since.

Believe it or not, I knew my husband's mother before I knew him. I was talking to my husband for three years over the computer on a dating site, Zeus. I met him through friends. I was helping friends move furniture out of their house and they asked him and a couple of their other friends to come over and help. I'm not one to have people sneak up behind me. I step back from pulling a couch up from the basement and I went to turn around and [my current husband was standing there]. I had my fists balled up because it was instant defense mode, and I turned around, looked, and was like okay, whatever. Then we started dating. We dated for a year and a half. We got to know each other. He proposed, and we were engaged for a year and a half. We got married August 5th of 2015 in Red Cloud.

He is from Idaho. He went from Idaho to Michigan, from Michigan to Kansas. His mom got remarried and she has lived in Red Cloud since he was six. He graduated from the high school in Red Cloud. [I was drawn to] how my kids were with him. He was more of a father to them than their own fathers were. We were just friends at the time and he has that father figure. It felt like I could have a relationship with him.

Suzanne, my oldest who is six, is a spitting image of me. She loves to swim. She loves to ride bikes. She's a little mini-me. Jonathan, who is five, is very lovable. He has a heart of gold. Someone can make him mad and he'll just look at them like, "You're just so rude" and then walk away. Then he'll come back and say, "I'm sorry for what I said," and give them a hug. Jace, he's two, is like his father. You can make him mad and he'll yell and then he'll walk up to them and start hugging on them [and say], "I'm sorry!" Selena, who is nine months, is full of energy. She is learning to walk. It's just crazy how they grow up so fast. I have my hands busy, but it's something I would never trade for the world. It's hard because I can remember from when I had all of them. It's crazy. It's like they were babies all at one time and now they're grown up.

We go out for walks. We like going to the Y and going swimming. We go for bike rides. We do movie nights on the weekends. We read books together and then we'll sit there. They have a chore chart and we go over the chores every night, and make sure they did their chores for the day. When they get home from school, they put a sticker on the chart. That's just something we do all the time. When it comes to movie night, we're all together on the bed, having popcorn and just chilling, watching a movie. [Some of their favorite movies are] *Beauty and the Beast*, *Shark Tales*, *The Nightmare Before Christmas*, *Hocus Pocus*, *Halloween Town*, *Pocahontas*, and *Coco*.

We try to have the tradition of going to church and doing things that go around our religion. With our church we'll sit there and read out of the Bible. My favorite [verse] out of the Bible is John 3:16. So we'll sit there, I'll read that, and we'll talk about what it means. Around Christmas, we'll put up the Christmas tree after Thanksgiving and every year, their first ornament they had, we put on the tree. [My children] love going to church. They're just like, "Mommy, when are we going back to church?" I say "Sunday, the day before Monday, before you go back to school," [and they say], "Okay!" Their friends go to church there too, so they love it.

[I try to raise my children with the values of] respect, honesty, and always respect yourself. Self-love comes first more than loving anyone else. Susie has had some problems with bullying. She's like, "Mommy, people are calling me ugly." I try to step up and I show her [she's not].

I look in the mirror and I'm like, "Suzanne, what do you see?"

She's like, "I see myself."

I'm like, "How do you see yourself?"

She's like, "I see myself as a pretty little girl."

I'm like, "It's because you are a pretty little girl."

With the respect we [say,] you need to stop and listen. You need to listen to what you're told. When someone goes to talk to us, I stop and then turn around and I give them eye contact because it teaches them eye contact and it's respectful.

[Hastings] is a place for a family to be at. There're things that you can do with your family. There're things that you can do on your own if you want to go out as a couple or by yourself. There're so many things to do here in Hastings. There's the Museum that you can do. There's the YMCA. There're multiple parks. There's Lincoln park up by the South McDonald's, there's a park behind the museum, and there's a splash park that's open during the summer. Then there's the water park. It's just a place that kids would love. During the summer, in August, they have Kool-Aid Days. [It] was my first [time going] this year. It was fun. Kool-Aid Days is definitely something to do with a family.

There is a parade. There're people who get in the Kool-Aid Man suit. Then there's people who guard Kool-Aid man. It's called the Kool-Aid crew. On Kool-Aid Days he rides on the back of a firetruck and they're giving out flyers telling everything what's going on during Kool-Aid Days. They have the prettiest baby contest. They have games for the kids. You can buy little tickets for them to do games. There's face painting. If you buy a Kool-Aid Day cup, which is two to four dollars, you get free Kool-Aid all day. Then after all those activities are done, on the next day they have stuff going on too. On Saturday they had the concert [and] fireworks. Kool-Aid man had to make an appearance at the concert. Then they do the boat races on Sunday and they run and all that. It's really cool. People come in from all over the place to come to Kool-Aid Days. My kids had a blast at Kool-Aid Days.

[Hastings] has changed our family's outlook a lot. We are getting stronger than what we were in Red Cloud. It's more peaceful than it [was in Red Cloud. There's a lot of] gossip with small towns.

[The people in Hastings] are very nice, respectful. There are a lot of kind-hearted people here. I've met a few people that have reached out and talked to us about helping with certain things. That's when I started going back to church because I needed to go back to church. That's what it was, I just needed get back into the church.

[The best thing about Hastings is] how there are so many things to do. There are so many different churches that you can go to. When you find that right one, you know that's where you are supposed to be. I enjoy that we have all of our seasons. It's just beautiful all year round. [My favorite seasons are] summer and fall. I was born in the winter and I loved it when I was a kid. Now, I hate the snow.

No, I have not [felt discriminated against in Hastings]. When I lived in Red Cloud, and I first went to go get a job, I was pregnant with my youngest, Selena. I was twenty-two weeks and I went to go in for an interview at Casey's and they were like, "Well, since you're twenty-two weeks pregnant, there's no point in hiring you." Here, they're not like that. They will give you a chance.

I honestly think Hastings is perfect the way it is. They post stuff when they have events coming up. There's a movie night coming up on Friday in the park, not too far from here. It is perfect the way it is. They are very hands-on with the community and I like that.

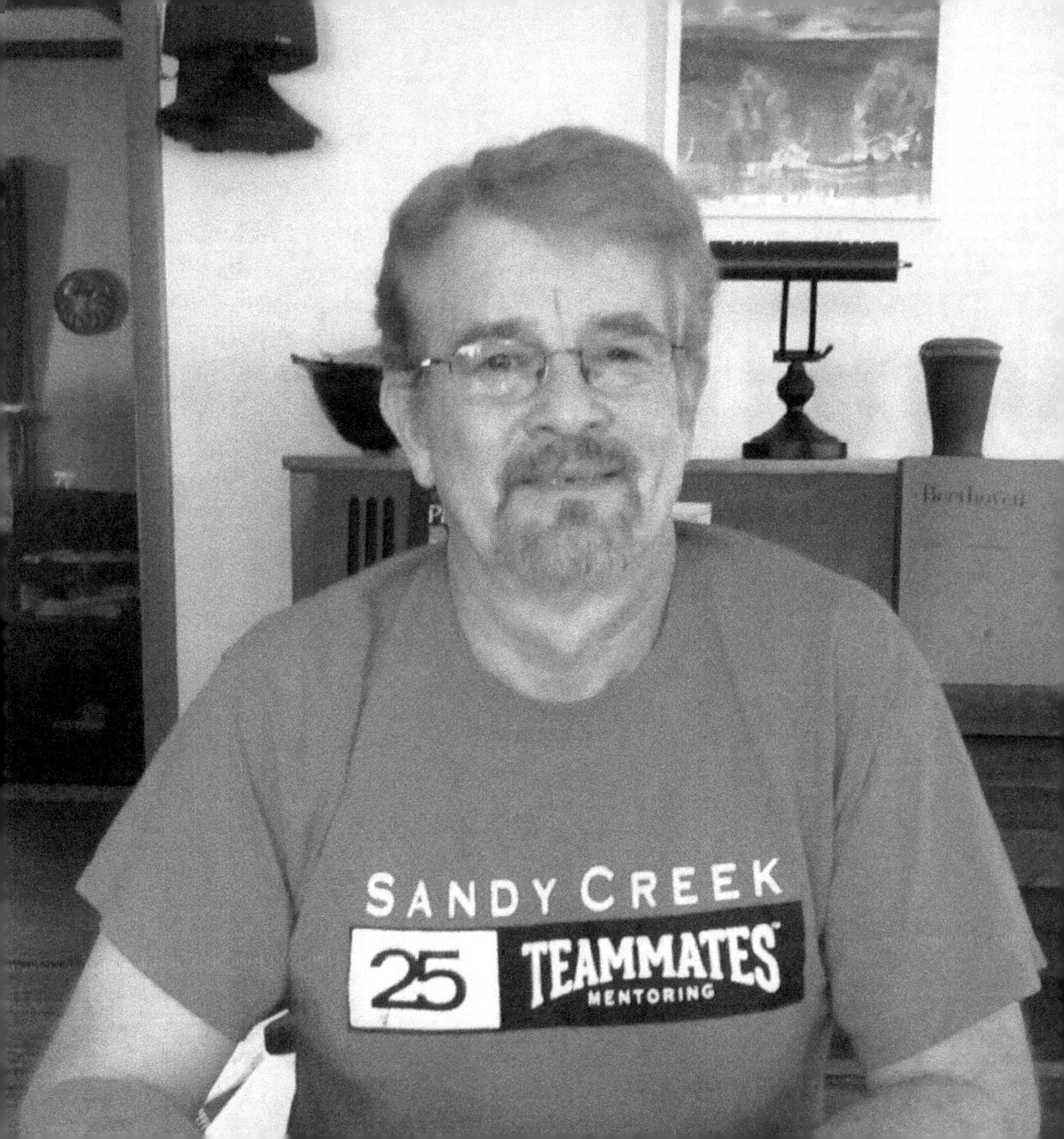
SANDY CREEK
25
TEAMMATES
MENTORING

I was born in Chadron, Nebraska. Then my family lived at Fort Robinson until I was in the ninth grade. In 1996 we moved to Hastings because my Dad worked for the Meat Animal Research [Center], at that time called Beef Research, and it was stationed at Fort Robinson and they moved it to Clay Center, and they found a house here in Hastings. Then I finished high school. One year at St. Cecilia's High then my junior/senior year at Hastings High School, the public school. Then went to Hastings College, studied music, and got a music degree in teaching, and until about four or five years ago I was teaching in public schools, mostly small schools in Nebraska. I'm a retired music teacher, also an organist at St. Mark Cathedral and I also play organ at St. Cecilia's Church and clarinet in Hastings Symphony. I'm not married, and I have no children.

I started piano lessons when I was seven years old. My parents made sure I got piano lessons. Then I had, when I was in fifth grade, I started playing in the band ... at Crawford High School or Crawford Elementary School and stayed in band through ninth grade.

ralph southern

Interviewed by Stratton Discoe

Then we moved here and stayed in band and around that time I was junior/senior year I took private lesson in clarinet. That is what I was doing, that was my extracurricular activities. Now, I would say that's my most predominant hobby.

I'm registered as independent [however] I tend to lean a bit to the liberal side. In my opinion, it just doesn't need to be definitive in all realms, I like that a lot. What I try to do is examine, if there's two candidates, what they believe and stand for, rather than the party. Sometimes I vote Republican, sometimes I vote Democrat.

For the past thirteen years, I've been a host parent for exchange students. It does in fact limit, you know, because they're teenagers, so they aren't just people I can turn loose. Right now, I have a boy from Bolivia and a boy from Germany. They're high school students here. The program I'm involved with is Student American International. The students stay for a full year. Hosting foreign exchange students is like a blind date too, you never know what you're going to get. I'm sure they [the students] obviously have an expectation when they come here based on stereotypes that probably aren't true. They always find that it's different because they see America through the scope of the pop-culture that's relevant now. Their orientation, they call it camp, it's not camp at all, it's in New York City. There goes any kind of preparation for living in Nebraska. All of them, that's counting this year's guys, there's twenty-two of them, have liked living here and going to school here. In the summers I've gone and visited them in their home countries. I've visited mostly Europe, and a little South America too. Austria, Spain, Germany, Czech Republic, and then Bolivia, Brazil.

My father's side, it would be my great-grandfather, William Southern, came from England. So that's the closest to being a [immigrant], as far as that goes. My grandmother was mostly German, and I don't know the exact [time], when that family came to the United States, but that was all in Iowa. On my mother's side, my grandfather was Scotch-Irish, and I don't know much beyond that. I mean, they came over from Ireland. Not anything directly [connected to Hastings], other than us remembering that. On my mother's side, up in Dawes County, which is where Chadron is, my great-great-grandparents came from Bohemia, and were homesteaders. They settled in the 1800s and there was nothing there except some trees, not even enough trees to build a house.

I grew up as a Catholic, and my mother didn't convert to Catholicism until about 1986/7. It was the year before her death. My dad was Catholic and from a Catholic family; he took me and my sister to Mass every Sunday. Around 1971, during my sophomore year at Hastings College, I became friends with one of the music majors [who] was Bahá'í. I also became friends with some theater people and one of those guys was a Bahá'í, he and his wife were Bahá'í. That's where it started out as far as hearing about it. At that time, in 1972/73 there were several students who, well, in Bahá'í terms, anything more than three is a lot, because we're so rare, and spread so thin around the world. At this time, I was still Catholic. So, there were probably five or six students all together, at Hastings College, that were Bahá'í, enough that we formed a club, a college club. There were also some adult Bahá'í's in the city of Hastings too. So that's where I first heard about it and in talking with my friends and discussing and then finally becoming a Bahá'í.

When it came right down to it, because I was Catholic, and I've been Catholic and believe in Jesus and what do I do? So, I was sitting in St. Cecilia's Church under one of the windows that had the Mother Mary in it, a stained glass window, saying Bahá'í prayers and this homeless guy came walking in. He had just fallen off a train and he was looking for help and he came to me. There were several other people in the church and you know, I was a college student, so I had about ten cents to my name at the time, and so I said, "You can go over to the priest's house," and it was kind of chilly outside. This is about 1970s, 1971, and I don't know exact dates, but that's about when it was. I leave, and he left and came back wearing a sweater, because I sent him over to the priest's house. Then they were hearing confession at the time, so he went over to confession and went up and knelt at the altar and prayed and then came back and shook my hand and thanked me. And I've been the whole time praying Bahá'í prayer. This was probably six months to a year of talking to my friends about it. That was probably the moment I fully committed to Bahá'í. The reason I mention the stained glass window with Virgin Mary is because it was either the very next Sunday or soon after I was attending Mass, when there use to be a monastery here, at what's now the Crosier Center, it was the Crosier Monastery, and that monastery was dedicated to Mary, and I was attending Mass and I received communion. I said okay Jesus, tell me, and there was no voice but just the feeling as I was receiving communion. I became convinced. Okay this is the, this is true. Now I only attend the Catholic Church when I play for Mass there. I'm an organist for their choir. Well, I don't want to say that it's just a job, because its more than that, but it's a paid position and so that's why. So, I attend Mass in that way, I probably wouldn't if … other than maybe special occasions, I always went to Mass with my parents, you know, on holidays for sure, and that sort of thing.

Bahá'í's basic belief is that there's one God. The three Onenesses: one god, one religion, and one humanity. Those are the onenesses, and the one religion is throughout history, from beginning until now. We believe God has sent messengers, and it's all the same path, but it's called different names by your culture, and where it came up throughout history. So, it might have a different name but it's still the same path. A different name meaning Hindu, Buddhist, or Muslim. From the outside it might look like that [a conglomerate of religions]; like we gathered together the teachings. From our viewpoint it's the same path but different times in history it would be called by a different name because it had a different messenger. The same basic spiritual teachings. Social teachings which change due to where they are in history or where they are in the world. Some of the details of like what you can eat or what you can wear or whatever might be specific to that time and place, but we look as one path. That's why each of the religions can say that they're the one path, because that's how it is. That's the absolute foundation. We believe all of the messengers of God, we call them manifestations of God, in a sense that when you are in their presence, it's like being in the presence of God. It's a channel. The unification of humanity is our goal. We all recognize that we are all one humanity and not divided by race or nationality or ethnicity. One of our sayings is, "unity with diversity," because we don't want everyone to be the same either, because that would be boring. When you go to a Bahá'í community in Africa, they're going to look and do things differently. The way they conduct themselves, to fit their culture and their background. One thing that unites us is being Bahá'í and believing in God, and that unites us, and we actually look for diversity, and the more different ways of doing things, the happier we are. The reason I was able to become Bahá'í was because I believed, and came to discover the belief that, the founder of the bahai faith Bahá'u'lláh, whose name means "the glory of God." The Báb was before him. It's pronounced Baab, that means the gate. And then Bahá'u'lláh was the founder of the Bahá'í faith. The Báb was the forerunner; similar to John the Baptist with Christ. Bahá'u'lláh went to prison and then had a revelation that he was messenger and the return of Christ.

Right now, [in Hastings] we're a very small community. There's two adults and their son and we get together periodically. This Saturday afternoon at 3pm they're hosting an interfaith devotional where we just say prayers from whatever faith they're in. Then as Bahá'í's, every nineteen days we have what's called a feast which is time for prayers and consultation and then usually some sort of fellowship. Right now, we meet in people's houses. Omaha has an actual building that's a Bahá'í center and there's a house of worship just north of Chicago. There's several continental houses of worship; there's one in Sydney, Australia, some of the countries, they're building what we're calling, "local house of worship." There's enough local Bahá'ís that they can build a house of worship.

I like it [Hastings], because aside from about six years right after I graduated college in 1973, I moved back to Hastings. I was away and then I came back. [During that time], one year I taught in a little tiny town down by Superior, Nebraska, for one year. Then their school was so small they merged with Superior. I was out of a job, so I moved to the Sandhills of Nebraska, to Arthur County, and I was there for five years. The people [in Hastings] that I know and interact and hang out with sometimes, [are] just nice people. Caring about issues and other people. They try to do things that help the larger community in some way. I haven't really run across any sort of persecution or anything. The closest that would ever come to that, and I wouldn't call it persecution, I would call it being concerned for my soul, was one of my more fundamentalist Christian friends, are really worried about what's happening to my soul because they feel I've rejected Jesus. So, it's for concern but they are not criticizing, they are praying for me. It's with goodwill, and there's tears in their eyes when they talk about it because they're so worried. I wouldn't call that persecution. I'm touched that they feel that strongly and they're worried about me.

josefa (bee) thomas

Interviewed by Brennin Leach

[I go by] Bee Thomas, or my real name is Josefa Thomas. I'm from the Philippines. I was a teacher in the Philippines. I taught in a parochial school run by Catholic missionaries. It was a big, big school where students wore uniforms. The teachers also wear uniforms. It was a really nice Catholic school. I taught there for eight years. Then I met my husband through pen pal. That's how I came to the United States. I have brothers and sisters. Actually, my mom and my dad were widow and widower [from before they were married]. On my father's side, I have three brothers and three sisters. That makes six. On my mother's side, I had three brothers, [but] they were already dead. My mom and my dad met, and they got married. I'm their only child. When I introduce my brothers and sisters, I don't call them half-brothers or half-sisters. We grew up under one roof, so we have that bonding and that love together. When I introduce them I just say, "This is my brother. This is my sister." I don't say half-brother or half-sister.

For first and second grade I went to the public school, and then one of my sisters was teaching at the

Catholic school, and she invited me to go to the parochial school where she was teaching. So, I did, and then she convinced me to be a Catholic, [but] I was baptized Methodist. I [there] went from third year [until I] graduated from St. Catherine's School. Then I went to the city to go to college, four and a half years of college. There's a college just for teachers, the National Teachers College. I went there. It was blessing in disguise. I told you, we didn't have means to go to college. But my father was a politician, and in the Philippines, the mayor is the king in the town. Politics play an important role. So, when this guy was running for mayor, my dad was the campaign manager, scheduling [the]campaigning. "Tonight, we'll go to Hallam, there will be a meeting there. Tomorrow we'll go to Edgar, there will be a meeting there at seven o'clock." That was my dad's job. He was at the mayor's house all the time because the mayor's house there are so many people, people just being there to listen and to support them. When the mayor won he gave my dad a job in return. Job opportunities are very rare there. He gave my dad a job for the term for mayor, four years. So, I was able to go to college for four years. How good can that be? It was a coincidence.

When I graduated there, I went to St. Catherine to my alma mater. At that time my employer, Father Julian, [said] there was no vacancy, but I was patient. He said, "Do you know how to type at a typewriter?"

I said, "Father, I don't." He said, "And well, why don't you go back to Manila, and I'll pay for your tuition fees and pay for all the expenses and after six months, you come back and report to me." Back then there were no computers. In six months, I learned how this and that. It helped me more. I could not have gone through six months [more] of typing. I could not have learned more. I memorized everything, period to comma and all that. So, he hired me.

    The school where I taught was a missionary school, so this priest sent mission letters to Belgium. Belgium is a Catholic dominant country. There are so many Catholics in Belgium, so he has so many benefactors in Belgium. These people send money to our school. From that he made improvements of the church. He made clinics. He made capital in every barrier, in little towns. He ran a higher catechism. He made use of the money that the people from Belgium sent. There were probably five of us that just did the typing. One letter cost a dime. You were paid by the letter. The first day I was hired, I only made fifteen or twenty letters and my coworkers they are just [going so fast]. So, I brought home a copy because it is in the Belgium language. I memorized everything from the period, the comma. You have to do the language, the spelling, from the period to the comma, everything. Boy I was really going fast. Then the last time I knew I was getting closer to $100 a day.

[Still,] every time I went to get my salary, because we didn't write checks, I always asked my employer and said, "Father, please remember me when you have a vacancy in your school because it's a big school. Please remember me." Every time I went, it never failed. My employer was a good priest. Sure enough when there was vacancy, he called me: "Josefa, I want you to be one of my teachers." Boy I jumped high. I remember those days and he was good to me, very nice. I thanked that priest. I was one of his teachers. I taught there for eight years until I met my husband. [Now] we're retired and enjoying life together. My husband is retired, and I'm retired too.

I was thirty years old when I met my husband, Terry. [Now,] it is forty years we will be together. I was a good girl. I'm very proud of that to tell my children, my two boys. I was a good girl [because] I never dated in my life. I never had a boyfriend, maybe due to poverty. I came from a poor family. My focus was to work hard. I was the only bread earner in the family. In the Philippines, they probably have nursing homes [now, but] when I was there, there were no nursing homes. I was a country girl. I was just focusing on working hard. I said to myself, "If I will marry somebody that [does] not have a job, I will just be hitting a nail on my head." So, I was very conscious, and I was really a good girl.

I never dated, never had a boyfriend until I met my husband. We didn't even date. We met over pen pal.

Back then, my coworker/friend Nora [and I], were both teaching in the same missionary Catholic High School. I was in the elementary and she was in the next building over, the high school. It was her free period, so she wasn't teaching at that time, but she was in her classroom. I got this message, "Will you come to my room?"

I answered her back said, "Sorry I cannot come I'm not feeling well. Can I see you this afternoon?" In the Philippines we don't feed the students, none of that kind of thing. We let the children go at 11:30am, and then they come back about 1:00pm or 1:30pm.

The same note came back, and she said, "Well if you are not interested, forget it."

I was interested [in] what she was going to tell me, so I walked to the next building. She was by herself and I entered her classroom. There were no students, just vacant chairs there. She was in front of the blackboard, sitting down and she threw me Terry's letter. Then, she said, "Read that." I read it and it was just simple, introducing himself. There was always something about God in his letters. After I read it Norris said, "Do you want me to introduce you to him?"

"If you want to…" That was my answer back.

At that time, Nora was receiving so many letters from around the world and she [couldn't] answer them all. She wrote a letter introducing me to Terry and at that time Terry got that. Terry sent her a thank you note thanking her for not throwing his letter in the trash but introducing him to somebody.

[Terry] wanted to have a bachelor life. He did not have a girlfriend. [He] worked as an accountant to the truck line [for] forty-eight years. [He] picked up the mail for their business and [his] personal mail. [He] came back to their office and of course threw [some] in the trash because [he] wasn't interested. [He] was bored that day and picked up this paper and said, "Well maybe I'd prefer writing a letter or two to send it in." [He] wrote four or five. [We got to know each other through them] and that is how we met.

I was brave. I was young, well, thirty years old. When you are poor, I'm still poor, but when you have that kind of life, you tend to look on the other side of the fence. You are curious, is the other yard greener over there? I was brave enough. I was young, and I wanted to see what was on the other side of the fence. If you look at the map of the Philippines, it is halfway around the world. I remember vividly, we don't have winter in the Philippines. When I landed there, I looked through the window of the airplane and it was raining. I could feel the airplane landing [with bounces and jolts]. My husband and I talked, back then there were no computers or cell phones, through the telephone: landline. He said, "In case of inclement weather, I could not come and meet you. Just call my boss's daughter who lives only fifteen minutes away from the airport." I just made up my mind. I said, "I'm not going to bother anybody. I'll just be at the airport and wait for my husband." Thank God, he was there.

The following day we went out, and San Francisco is [a] very cold place. It was 55°F and I was shivering. I was cold. [Back home,] we don't have heavy snow. I thought that the coldest place I've ever been was 55°F. I was wearing my skin blouse and open shoes. I was embarrassed to complain to my husband because we just got married. We met in December and then exchanged letters. Then we got married. There was really no acquaintance because after the wedding, they left for the United States. There was no knowing each other as acquaintances. We got married, they left, and then here I came [in] the United States. He met me in San Francisco.

He took me to the Golden Gate [Bridge]. We rode the boat there and if I close my eyes ... he was by the deck with this yellow shirt. Here I was, my knees trembling. I said, "How can I complain?" I was embarrassed to complain, [but] by the water it was so cold. I finally could not stand it. So, I said, "I'm cold." He took me to Macy's, a big department store, [and] bought me a coat. At first I selected a red sweater since it was kind of around Valentine's Day. I think I came in on February 13th. I was embarrassed to let him spend money for me. We are already husband and wife, embarrassing. I just wanted a sweater, so we bought this sweater for me. As soon as we went out of Macy's, I was already shivering. [We went back in and he] bought me a coat. That was my first coat. It was heavier than me. It [was] suede. It was heavy. He told me, "If you are cold [now], it is so much colder in Nebraska." Sure enough, when we got to Nebraska it was below zero, quite an initiation for me. It was -15°F and his car wouldn't even start.

When I first came here, I did not work right away because I did not know how to drive. It's a necessity to drive. But then my husband was so understanding. He asked me to learn how to drive, and I did learn how to drive. [I] had a few escapades with the trees. Anyway, I sat down together and said, "Whoever is not earning more will stay home." I did not argue, so I took care of my children. The school was just right there. They did not want to eat in the school. They wanted to come home. I looked through the window, "Bye, Winston! Love you! Stay away from trouble!" Then they come home especially in the wintertime and it's cold and windy that they want to eat here. They want to come home because there's warm soup waiting for them. I looked through the window. If my son is walking, I go in the kitchen and wrap the bowl, so it was not too hot. I'm a spoiler, but they remember those things. Those little things, my children will remember. Even now that they're big, when I passed by the room and their feet are sticking out, I cover. I meet my children and then I'll hug them and then when they sit, sit down here on this heating pad. That's warm you know, that's warm. Then I put the heating pad on their lap. I put their coat on the furnace, so by the time they go back to school it is warm. You know, those little things. Remember those little things, the love that you give to your children. I'm not bragging, [but] they call us every day. No fail. One is in Missouri and one is in Minnesota. The love that you plant on them, the love that you give to somebody, will really stay if it is genuine.

Going back to where I work. I did not work for a while. Then I decided to go to school to be a nurse, LPN. I did good, I did. I got eighth in my clinicals but then I was beginning to forget my family. I was beginning to be away from my family. I [would] get up early in the morning and go to school. You have to be there early when I had my clinicals. I have to report there at six o'clock in Aurora and then come home late, about 8:30–9:00am. I would just say, "Hi, guys. Hi, guys," and then run down the basement and study. I was beginning to forget the bonding that I have with my family. I learned many things about nursing and I am still doing it with my family. It didn't go to waste because I stayed. I studied hard. When I work, I really like to work hard, my best. And then when I go to work, I like to be professional. One day I came home, and I got my bag and I came in and I just sat down. I'm tired. In front of me was a newspaper. Good Sam[aritan Village] was looking for an activities person and I said, "That sounds like an interesting one." I went to apply, and they took me right away. So that began my journey at Good Sam.

Good Sam is a nice place to work. I work with the elderly and the babies. The babies, I treated them like my own, like my very own. I was nominated Employee of the Month. I got Employee of the Year. Not everybody gets to appear here. Coworkers voted for Employee of the Year. You have the plaque that says Employee of the Month parking, the whole month. Then for your Employee of the Year, you have one-year parking space. Nobody can park there except for the Employee of the Year. That's nice. Then they nominated me to the Nebraska Health Care Association. I got second place on that. At Good Sam they nominated me for the award of the whole company. Good Sam is a big, big company. I didn't win, but it was an honor to just be nominated. Before I left Good Sam, I was nominated again for Employee of the Month. I was nominated by the YWCA women's in Hastings. I was nominated [for] woman of the year. I got some awards there. This was just about your professional etiquette and how you work. They had a Good Sam, where I was working. If you clock in one minute late, you're out of the game. [I] was always on top of that for five or six successive years. I got an award for that. I belong to the Phi Beta Kappa at Central Community College. I don't call in sick. Except the very last one. My children were still here with us and I ate the wrong thing. The following day I was throwing up and my two boys were standing by the bathroom door: "What time is it now? I still want to go to work."

"Mom, no, that business can go on without you."

But my dedication, sincerity, and loyalty were there. When you work, work hard. Give it all you got. My advice to you. There's one thing that you will remember from [me,] to work hard.

[Before then,] when the boys were little, I was a stay-at-home mom. Terry's mom was here, my mother-in-law. Grandma was here. She lived with us for almost twenty-five years. My friends said, "You mean you live with your mother-in-law? When my mother-in-law comes to visit me, after two or three days I'm ready to get rid of her." But it is our culture. We take care of our old people and you don't. I think now they are learning because of the different cultures merging in the United States. I think they are learning, and they are learning to take care of their older people instead of sending them to the nursing homes right away.

They take care of them. I remember vividly after our wedding. Terry and [his] mom evidently planned that when they come to the United States because [him], his mom, and grandma were just to be living here by themselves, three of them. Then grandma died and there were just two of you. The day after the wedding, there's grandma [mother-in-law] standing in front of me. She said, "When you come to the United States, I will be moving out," like it was a slap in the face. I didn't understand your culture. I didn't know your culture. I didn't know back then. I had tears. I said, "How come? Why?" And her answer was, "To give privacy to the newlyweds." Privacy! You could get lost here!

When we go to the United States, [Terry] owned a building downtown, [his] mom was going to go there. I held her hands. I said, "No. I want you to stay." Thank god she did. She stayed, and [Terry] got rental property instead of [his] mom. That's a plus, because we have two boys. Every time they came home, they looked for grandma. They gave a kiss to grandma. When we have a prayer, a shared prayer, we always hold hands and they always pray for grandma. They never fail to go to the cemetery. No fail, every day. They're very, very close to their grandma. That's my advice, be nice to your grandma.

My dad and my other relatives didn't want me to marry an American because they said, "Us Filipinos don't have divorce." This is exactly what my dad said: "When you go there, they will just divorce you, and you will be like a lost bird in the woods. You don't know anybody there. You don't have any relatives there." My fear was [of what] we read in the papers about discrimination, American discrimination, all the time. I was scared that they would just discriminate [against] me. I hear of people discriminating. We read in the papers about discrimination. That's when my mom and my dad especially said that they will divorce you or they will discriminate [against] you. But, I haven't met anybody yet that discriminated [against] me. I think it depends on the person, if you talk to them, I am always the first person to talk to somebody. I always start the conversation. In fact, if we go to a grocery store or Walmart, my youngest one would say, "Mom, I bet you $10 you will know somebody here," and sure enough, I did. I take time. I don't just say, "Hi!" I take time to say hello, [to] stop. We live in a busy society where everybody is on the go, go, go. Everybody is so busy, so stop and talk to a friend. Hop on the telephone [and] say, "Hello! How are you?" [We're] just so busy we don't have time to smell the flowers. That's why, in the spring and summer, we have a big garden. We always have a big flower garden and a big vegetable garden, and we give them to people. We invite people that we know don't have a garden and then we let them enjoy picking different vegetables. After that, we visit on the patio. Take time, talk to a friend. Let them know that they are important. Again, I haven't met anybody that discriminated [against] me, thank the Lord. It depends upon the person, if you are approachable or friendly.

[Other than that, when I decided to move here,] I just did not think. I was just so excited. I told you the truth, that I want to see the other side of the fence. When you're poor, there were times at night we didn't even [eat]. Rice is our staple food; our main food and we sometimes take the bacon grease. Here that's not, you know, you have to throw that. It blocks or plugs the arteries. But there, as long as we had rice, fluffy rice with the bacon grease and put the fish sauce or salt, that's just perfect! My sister would send me to the market and say number one would be bones, and the bones do not even have meat. It was mainly bones. We boil that and [add] vegetables, like carrots and potatoes. The whole family would eat that, as long as there is an aroma of the food [bones]. Coming to the United States I gave everything away: my clothes, my sisters, my friends, my belongings. Our house was made of bamboo and a grass roof. It was a nipa hut. Our house was like that. Every time I received my salary, which was not much, I got concrete [that I] stuck in there until I had enough to make a hollow block around our house. "Little by little," I said, "I would improve our house." So, we did. Then I had a television. It's hard to buy those things because they are expensive. I had a sofa and little things. I told my sister-in-law, "All these things and the house will be yours on one condition. I want you to take good care of my mom and my dad. And this will all be yours. Nothing is precious to me, as long as you take good care of my mom and my dad." And she did. That was our agreement. She did, so she still owns my house. Nothing is precious to me.

[When I came to the US,] I had so many changes. [Especially] with the climate. When I told you, we don't have snow or winter we only have dry and wet season. When we add the wet, we call it the monsoon season. It dries, it drains, and it quits. It rains, and it gets where you cannot plan for an outdoor event, because for the season it's wet and muddy. Then when it's dry, it's dry, no rain. It's so hot. I lived in the valley. So, I really did not have electricity when I was there. I think now my town has electricity, but when I was there we didn't. When it [was a] full moon [and] we were little, we got [to go] out. It's really nice, [a] full moon, [when] you don't have electricity. We'd go out and play and play and people would go out just go walking. They enjoy walking.

The food [is also different]. We have our own food that I like. Here, my husband is a meat eater. For me, because I came from a big family and meat is very expensive [in the Philippines, I am content] as long as there is an aroma in my food. I told you there's no meat, the bone is the aroma. The flavor of the meat can feed about 10 people, Here, one big piece can just go for one person, like the prime rib. When we just got married, my husband said, "Where is your meat?"

"Well I made it into a stir fry and had it for supper and I can still have some for tomorrow." Young Americans, they just get that one tonight and that's about it. Me? I eat it and I have some more for the following day.

The people changed. I miss my friends. I had so many friends in the Philippines, had so many friends. Again, I did not have a hard time finding friends here because I communicate with people and I take a minute or two. The other day, Saturday, we were at Allen's and I saw this young mother and daughter. I stopped to say hello, because when the younger girl was a baby I saw them she wanted to come to me. So, she came to me. I walked with her in the aisle and then when they were leaving, the [family] wanted her [back] and then the baby did not want to go back to them. We laughed because [we] remembered that time. People like you by the way you treat them. It's a two-way street. If you're nice to people, they are also nice to you. It's a two-way street.

My first impression of the United States is like a tree planted on a good soil, on a fertile soil. America is a nice country, very nice country, but some people they take it for granted. They don't realize the opportunity that they have. [When I came it this country, I expected] it would be a nice place to live in. That's why people always like to come here. That's why, when some of my friends come, they don't even want to go back home. Because it's nice. It's a nice country. America is supposed to be number one in the world. All the countries look up to America. If you see the American flag, it's just so nice. When I became an American, I asked my husband for an American flag. We have a flag pole. Just lately, we have those half bunting flags on the railing of the roof of our house. Then when my children came, they said not to be climbing on the roof. That's the last time they let somebody up there. Mom don't be climbing on the roof. You can decorate anything. You can just put it here on the fence, mom. But I like America. I like the flag. You know, to show that you're American. You're an American.

My [other] expectations well, like laundry. Very easy to wash. I told my relatives, my mom and my dad, "Now you just wash it for ten or thirty minutes." We washed it for the whole day [in the Philippines]. My mom and I would go to the river with a basin or tub full [of laundry] and wash clothes. [We'd] put it under in the river and we'd dry it on the big rocks. When it dries, and we would fold them and go home. I remember those days. If you didn't go through that kind of life, you will not know the difference. I went through that and I went through this. I can compare which life is better. I remember those days. My mom and my dad would go in the river after washing all the clothes. We'd take a bath in the river, swimming with the fish. [Some] other changes ... we didn't have running water. We had a pump well. We didn't have the hot water, or we don't have a heater. If you want to take a bath, we had to boil water, make it hot, and pour it on our water pot to take a bath.

Here, especially when you're in a hurry, you just turn on the stove and then you're cooking. But in my home, especially when the wood was wet, we had wood stove, it's hard to start a fire when you're in a hurry. Sometimes we don't have wood and we go to the dump and I always say, "Awe, guys, if you are in the Philippines in my home, this would be very useful to throw those. Why would you put it in the dumpster, in the dump?" It is so hard to throw things. I know that sometimes when I see something that is salvageable, I'll bring it home. I still have that Filipino attitude. I still have the Filipino blood running in my veins, because I experienced that. I know what life is.

We garden a lot. We have a big flower garden and a big vegetable garden. More than fifty tomatoes. And peaches, lots of them, and we just want to share. We invite people to come and pick and then we fellowship in the garden. We always have company. We play cards. We invite somebody and then I prepare door prizes. They put their name in the sack and [Terry] will draw names. They're like little kids. They hope [we] will [call their] name. I like to see them smile, to see them happy. I like that. I also cook something, but if they would like to bring something I welcome them. That's one of the things that I enjoy.

My husband is always scared about when I see that somebody needs help on the road. It comes naturally. I just pull over and just help that person. My husband said, "That's dangerous." Someday it will be snowing [and] it's always nice to put a little shovel in your car, or blanket in your car. Because if you see somebody bleeding along the road ... oh well the other day we were parked at IGA. There was a car parked right on our side. When we were going inside I said, "Guys, do you need help?" Now the other one was facing together. He was trying to restart the car. Before I got inside the car, I saw this guy pour some liquid inside the engine. Then the owner of the car went inside and started it. It started a fire, and he was inside the car. I was worried. I opened the trunk. I opened his trunk just to look if there was a rag to smother the fire and I didn't see any rag. So, I hollered at that guy next door in the pickup and he told them what to do. And they were able to put out the fire. The young man had a fire extinguisher. It's always nice to be prepared. I'm one of those [people that] if somebody was in the ditch, I would stop, especially in the snow time. You know those little things, deed for the day.

Well, at present, I am sixty-six years old. I'm on the Adams County Board of Supervisors ... that's the room that we're in here today. This is where we meet twice a month. I also own a business in Hastings called Denmar Corporation, which I've had for over forty years. That was my main line of work until I became a supervisor approximately eight to ten years ago. I'm married and have four children: three daughters and one son. Three of them still live in Hastings. My daughter just graduated from Hastings College and now she works with HHS. She has very beautiful red hair. My son works for a company called T&L Irrigation. He quite often travels overseas, he's out of the country quite a bit. I have a daughter who works with teenage mothers in Hastings. She's been involved in STARS program and different programs with the county.

I was born in a small town called Minden, Nebraska, and when I was born we moved to Hastings. I have three brothers, two of those who are born in Minden and my younger brother was born here. If I remember right, it was a job opportunity for my dad.

Interviewed by Abigail Olson

scott thomsen

He had been in the Navy, learned the trade of being a mechanic in the Navy. He came here and started his own shop called Tenasaw the Clinic. That's why they moved. It's either that or they want to get away from my mom's parents. One of the two. Both my parents were from Minden and I was really close to my mom's parents, my grandparents. They were farmers that came from Denmark. My grandfather was an influential man. In Nebraska, back in the Depression days, stories were told how he helped a lot of the other residents in Minden survive through the tough times. They were very traditional, very strict upbringing, which I think my mother got from them because she was very strict with us as we were growing up too. The other side, my dad's parents were a lot easier going but I was never very close to them. They passed at a very young age, so I don't have a lot of information to share about that.

There was a time about ten years ago, I thought I was getting too old to climb ladders all day long. Therefore, I took a position with another company and I was selling materials that I had used for thirty some years, and Broken Bow was part of my territory. That was a neat little town and it reminded me of Minden, Nebraska. I had an uncle in Minden who owned a farm. Every summer, during high school, my brothers and I would go work with him because he had no children. He always wanted to turn it over to one of us. When you're eighteen, who wants to be a farmer and live in Minden, Nebraska? It makes no sense at all. I would have loved to have done that because I love farming, but that just wasn't cool back then.

I spent a couple years at a community college. They had a basketball program at that time. I had gotten into some trouble in Hastings. I was going to go to the University of Nebraska. I had some issues here, which didn't really allow me to go to UNL. I got a scholarship to go to CCC to play basketball. I wasn't really interested in school at that time. I was kind of a dumbass at that age. But I went there, and I spent two years there. I don't even think I had enough credit for a one-year degree. I played basketball and drank. I was going to be an accountant. I always enjoyed working with numbers; that's one of the few things that I did enjoy doing in school but I just I didn't put any effort into it. I did learn enough that in all the years that I've had my company, I've done all my own books and taxes and everything so that what little I did learn did pay off.

Well, after I then, I dropped out of there. After my second year of basketball was done. It was only a two-year school and there was a coach in Seward for Concordia that was interested in me playing basketball with them. I moved to Lincoln to be closer. It just so happened that that coach got fired. The new coach didn't know anything about me. I wasn't offered a scholarship which wouldn't have done me any good anyhow, I just would have gone there to play basketball. I stayed in Lincoln for the next five years, and I worked at a meatpacking plant, which was actually a very good-paying job for Lincoln at that time, if you were just a grunt and had no education, and a lot of the football players from the university work there too. So, I got to know them. They were a bunch of drunks and druggies too, so it worked out great. Mostly all I did in Lincoln was work, drink, and do drugs. I was a full-fledged alcoholic and drug addict by that time. I was kind of on a downward spiral. I needed to get out of that town. I moved back to Hastings; that's when I got a job at the regional center. I stayed there for five years and didn't really grow up any, but I calmed down.

    I was working for the state out at the Hastings Regional Center, I had been there for five years. I worked on the psych wards and I oversaw my own ward up there. It was a great job and I loved it to death. The state just didn't pay enough to buy a house, buy a car, and raise a family. I needed to find something else to do to make a little bit more money because I had just gotten married. There was somebody else that worked [there] and he knew how to do roofing. I helped him a few times. We thought let's just start our own business. We signed up enough jobs that we thought we could afford to leave the security of working for the state. We named our company Denmar. My wife at that time was named

Denise and his wife was Mary, and that's how we got Denmar. It was better than Thompson Siding, or Smith Construction, or something like that. This was kind of catchy. It wasn't original because Pamida stores, named that company after [the owner] three children, Pam, Mike, and David. It was kind of interesting. That's how we came up with the name, and it just kept getting bigger all the time. I didn't work or play well with others. My partner lasted a year. I enjoyed the physical aspects of the job. I always did like to work, I was never afraid of work. I just put everything I had into it and grew all the time. It's almost as old as my oldest child. It's like I have five kids I raised. I still do jobs for Denmar. My kids aren't as thrilled about physical labor as I was, so none of them have chosen to take it over. Although it's a standing joke that it's always there if they want it. I'll just keep working as long as I can. But nowadays, I just kind of pick and choose what I want to do. I say no to people, where I never used to do that before. If it's not something that physically I can do, or something I even want to do. There's no expansion in the future.

I'm a member of the First Presbyterian Church, have been for many years. When I was young, I went to Sunday School there and have not been really active but have been a member there for a long time. Like I said, the Adams County Board of Supervisors, I'm a Republican, although parties don't mean a whole lot to me. When I decided to run for this office, the main reason I registered as a Republican was every two out of three voters in Adams County are Republican. If you want to get elected to something, it's beneficial to be a Republican. Of course, I'm on a wide array of boards [including] boards of directors here in Hastings also.

There was an opening and somebody who was on the Board of Supervisors saw me one day and brought it up. On a certain date you could put your name in and they would interview potential candidates. There's a clerk of the district court, the county clerk, and county attorney; those three review prospective clients; they choose who they think would be a good supervisor. It interested me, there wasn't very much money involved in the position, but it just intrigued me. At that time, I wasn't as young as I used to be, and I thought this would get me off the ladders because I climb ladders all day long. So, I put my name in the ring and they interviewed, and I was surprised, but they chose me to be a supervisor. I've been elected the next two times.

I've had a few wives. I met my first wife there [the regional center], she was the love of my life, but it only lasted a year and a half. I was very immature, drank a lot and did a lot of drugs. That kind of spelled the end of that marriage. I wasn't fit to be around anybody at that time. There was a high turnover of people my age there. There were very few men and there were a lot of ladies that worked out there. My second wife also worked out there and we got married very briefly. She was pregnant, and we were married for several years. She had a daughter that was three that I adopted and then we had a son right away. It was a nice thing for a little while. After maybe ten years, she was kind of fed up with all the drinking and drugging. I had a very contentious divorce that split up the family. I was single again, but by then I had my own business and I was making more money. One day I went to buy a new car and there was this pretty girl that worked at the dealership. I made sure that she was the one that waited on me. There was a car there I really like but they didn't ever want to give me a good deal on it. I remember telling her that well, I will buy this car from you, if you'll go out with me. She screwed up and said yes.

    We dated for a long time, we moved in together. She lived in Grand Island, she moved back here, she got tired of my drinking in a hurry, and she moved back to Grand Island. I went to rehab, and we ended up getting back together and got married. She was a lot younger than me, and she never had any children. She always wanted to have children, but we tried for a long time and could never have any. I already had kids, so I wasn't overly excited about having any more. We decided to go the adoption route. We went to Nebraska Children's Home, and at my age I didn't think they would ever give us a kid. Nonetheless, we had to fill out questionnaires. There was something I wrote in there that this young lady that was going to have a baby, it just struck her as this is who I want to raise my child. They called us one night and we went to get her from the hospital the next morning. We brought home a baby girl. About three or four months later, I came home, and my wife had this shit-eating grin on her face. I knew right away that she was pregnant. So, we had two kids in a hurry. She was really happy and everything. She filed for divorce too, because I was still drinking and drugging. I tried treatment again, and she gave me another chance. I celebrated seventeen years sober in August. We've been married, well, sh—since 1990. You do the math, long time, I say. If I wouldn't have quit drinking, we wouldn't have been married. I've seen it wreck too many lives and break up too many families and stuff. We're still together, pretty happy.

I've tried to establish family traditions with my children. Not all they appreciate, but you get things from your parents, not everything you want to get from them. If you grew up with your parents, you'll get things from them, some good and some bad. We didn't have very much money at all, but there were a few times where we did take a vacation. If I remembered something we did from when I was young, I would try to do that with my kids. I remember going to the Black Hills when I was young and it being a happy memory. My oldest child is forty-five, and my son is forty-one, I think. I have twenty-one and twenty-year-old girls or twenty-two and twenty one—whatever the hell—they're kind of spread apart. I've done that with each set of kids. We were able to do a lot more than I was able to do when I was young. Traditions, there's less and less of it as each generation goes by. I think that's common place when I was young. We always had huge family gatherings, and there were nuclear families. It's harder and harder to do right. We make sure our families get together for the big occasions. My youngest daughter's getting married next year. We will be going out to Connecticut, where they want to get married. The traditions are trying to keep the families together. Cousins grew up knowing each other and things like that. I really don't know my three brother's kids that well. But, that's my own fault.

    The one thing I'm proud of is my kids have good work ethic. They've gotten that from me, because I work way too much, work seven days a week, quite often. They don't always come to me with their hand out wanting more money. It's kind of hard with two sets of kids; it's different parts of the family. My younger kids didn't grow up with their older brother and sister. That's always been a thing that I keep trying to work at. The two older ones have a connection and the two younger ones have a connection but the four of them being brothers and sisters, that's been a challenge. But as they all get older, some of the petty issues that they had have kind of went away. I've tried to be a better example to my second batch of kids than I was with my first kids who grew up with an alcoholic.

My kids all have opportunities to go elsewhere but three out of four of them have stayed. My twenty-two-year-old is in Las Vegas right now; I don't know how long she'll be there. She's the only one that hasn't graduated college. As she gets a little bit older, she's realizing that she wants to go back to school someday. After high school she went to a travel academy, to either work on cruise ships or be a flight attendant or something like that. She went there and graduated; she just flew right through it. She got offered a job in North Carolina but turned it down to become a waitress. I think she was afraid to go that far away. She's a beautiful girl physically and she's got such a way with people that she makes a fortune working in bars. She'll save up $10,000–15,000, and she's living on her own. She'll live on her own and save up a bunch of money. Then she'll travel for a while to South America. She was in Bangkok, Thailand, for, I think, six months. She does this every year and she does all this on her own, which just scares the shit out of me because I'm not Liam Neeson. I can't go over and save her if she gets taken, but that's what she does. The other three are still here, although my youngest will leave sooner or later. My wife's family, well the family she has left. Every year after we got married, she would always go back to Connecticut and see her family. That's where her parents and her sisters lived. Every year, for the best twenty years, she took the two youngest that we had with her. My youngest has went out there and she just kind of fell in love with it. She wanted to get married somewhere other than boring Hastings, Nebraska. Connecticut is kind of a pretty place, so that's where they're going to get married.

Hastings is boring. I guess that's why they invented airplanes, cars, and stuff. So, you can easily go somewhere for entertainment. In Hastings, you can grow up relatively crime free, which is a big deal especially as it seems like the world is changing all the time. In Hastings, there's just a lot of common folk, a lot of common sense, which is good. People still know people. People are still trying to be in everybody's business but it's a good community. There are two sides of Hastings too. I know this from my past and from working with the Drug Task Force in Hastings. After midnight Hastings is a totally different town. Considering my background, I work with a lot of groups called ASAAP, which stands for Area Substance and Alcohol Abuse Prevention, and Horizon—they treat alcoholics and drug addicts. There's still that [substance abuse] around here, but for the most part it's in the bigger cities. When I lived in Lincoln I was dealing drugs out there because it's readily available. If I would have went to the University of Nebraska, I would more than likely be dead today because I was going to live in Harper Hall. If you've ever heard of

Harper Hall, back then, when I was young, that was the drug capital of Nebraska. You can raise a family here; we have a lot of parks, a lot of nice people. It's clean, but it's boring. Sometimes that's not always good. Nonetheless, people still have decent values and morals for the most part. I think everybody wants to instill that in their own children and there's no better way to learn than from example. I think it's a good place.

When I was young, there weren't many black people here. The few that were here played basketball and they were good too, so I got to know them. We were real friends. When I married, my first wife, we got married up in Montana on top of a mountain. It was her, a friend of mine who was black, another girl, and me. We dropped him off in eastern Montana because he had a child up there. Then he took a bus to meet us up in the mountains. He was scared to death, because there were only cowboys in Montana back then, and they did not like black people. I saw that people in town would just stand and stare at him. When I grew up, to tell you the truth, I don't recall any Hispanics in Hastings. Now there's a lot of Hispanics in Hastings. I'm also the teen court judge for here. We just had teen court yesterday. I see a lot of Hispanics come through that. Hastings is becoming more and more diverse all the time.

I don't openly see it [discrimination], but the people that I associate with and deal with aren't that kind of people. I'm sure it happens but

I don't see it happen. I think people are a lot more accepting than when I grew up. I think people are always trying to find fault in others. I mean, Megyn Kelly, I just heard about this. She was talking about something in the past and just happened to mention blackface and it's almost like they don't hear what you say. They're just waiting for you to say something that they can cut you down on to try to make themselves look better than you. That's another issue that just pisses me off anymore. If somebody doesn't feel good about themselves, the only way they can get up is to bring you down here. That's just a horrible thing. The ASAAP group that I work with, I go to schools. I have gone to schools to talk about my addiction and talk about bullying to try to help with that.

I think it's all up to your generation [to make Hastings a more unified community]. There're no easy answers at all. It's awareness. It's acceptance. And there's much more awareness today, that people, they just must be more accepting of people. I'm not so sure that our president today is helping that a whole lot. Although I voted for him. I must admit that, some of the things that he says and does, and part of that is that I have mixed feelings on the Caravan. That's, you know, I have a lot of mixed feelings on that. I don't think how he's bringing it to the public is fair. So now, there's no easy answers. I wish I had the answers. I would've solved this problem a long time ago. Now you work on it.

My English name is Stella. My real name is Siying. I'm from China, and I moved to the United States with my husband in July 2017. I am from Guangdong province, which is the Cantonese area in southern China. I grew up in the coastal city of Zhanjiang, which has about 7 million people, and then I went to university in Beijing, which is the capital city of China.

After university, I moved back to Guangdong and lived in multiple cities for work. I come from a relatively poor working-class family. My parents did not go to high school, and they didn't have a lot of money. When I was a kid, we lived in a three-bedroom apartment with my grandma and my uncle's family. There were seven people living in the small apartment. My immediate family moved to another apartment within the same neighborhood when I was in middle school. My parents were born in China in the 1950s. China had just finished a civil war and it was a very difficult time for many people. It was right after World War II, and the whole country had basically been destroyed. My parents grew up in my hometown of Zhanjiang. Most

siying (stella) wu

Interviewed by Ben LeBar

people in the country were living in poverty at that time. I don't remember the exact statistics, but I think more than 95 percent of people were living on about $2 a day at that time.

Although my family was poor, I did well in school. I was able to attend the University of International Business and Economics and major in public administration. The school is in Beijing, the capital city, and it was very hard to get into. Due to the large population, the competition for university is very fierce. I have always liked school, and the friends I made along the way have always helped with the education process.

I speak two dialects of Chinese, Cantonese and Mandarin. Cantonese is my first language, so I grew up speaking that at home. I learned Mandarin because it is used in school. I started learning English at the age of 10, as it was a required course in school. It is also a part of the college entrance exam, so it is necessary to get good grades in English to go to a good university in China. After I moved to Hastings, I started learning Spanish through a local church. The class is free and basic. I have made some friends in the Spanish class, as a lot of it is just people getting together to talk and hang out. Although I have learned a lot, it is so difficult to learn yet another language.

My husband is originally from Hastings and we have been married for almost three years. We met in Shenzhen, China, where he was teaching English at the time. He lived in China for six years, so he has a good sense of Chinese culture. I think he is different than many people in America in that he is very openminded.

Holidays are an important part of Chinese culture, as it is a time for families to reunite. My husband and I don't really celebrate many American holidays, other than Thanksgiving and Christmas. We don't celebrate Chinese customs here either. Part of the reason is because a lot of the festivals in China are associated with food, and the food is not very easy to make. I just got back from China for the Mid-Autumn Festival in September. The moon is supposed to be the brightest and fullest at that time of the year, so it's a symbol of family togetherness. I also went back to China for the Spring Festival. The Spring Festival is the beginning of the lunar year and it's also a celebration of the year that has just passed. Here, when we celebrate Chinese holidays, it's just me and my husband. I don't think there are many Chinese people in Hastings, other than the people who work at the Chinese restaurants. There are not even many Asians.

I work with my husband running his family's business. They own apartments, and I do the bookkeeping. I also have a part-time job at an accounting firm. I have a strong business background from when I was in China. After graduation, I worked for seven years in retail management with a few international companies. Right now, there are not a lot of opportunities to use my degree. My job here is not very difficult compared to what I used to do.

My husband is from Hastings, and I came here a couple of times before we got married in 2016. I noticed a lot of differences here than in China, especially with how quieter it is than in China. I had to make a lot of adjustments when I came to Hastings. I didn't drive at all in China, so I had to learn how to drive. I got my driver's license last December, but I'm still a very new driver. There are so many people in China, so drivers tend to be more aggressive on the roads. You kind of have to fight your way into traffic. If there's a gap between cars, then you have to go, otherwise you will have to wait for a long time. There is a lot of traffic, so we often use public transportation, subways and buses mostly. Very few people own cars in China. Cars are expensive and public transportation is actually pretty good in China, especially in the cities. The countryside is, however, a different story. One in fifteen or sixteen people own a car in China, not like here where you must have a car to get around.

It is very cold here, not like where I grew up, which is in a tropical area. There are a lot of differences and similarities from where I grew up, but I think people pretty much have the same needs and want the same things. They want good jobs, good housing, and a good healthcare plan. The biggest difference is that we have different ways of doing things. For example, let's say the education system. The educational environment I grew up in is very competitive because of the large population, so you have to fight for everything. You must get really, really good grades on the entrance exams in order to go to a good school. That is why there is so much emphasis on exams in China. Another difference is that good schools in China are usually public. I assume private schools, like Hastings College, are generally better in America. Private schools in China are generally considered to be worse, as they tend to be for kids who cannot get into public schools.

A difference between my hometown and Hastings is that the people are friendlier and more talkative with strangers here. The best thing about Hastings is that the people are very friendly. Hastings is a very quiet and peaceful small town. A lot quieter compared to my hometown. I know a lot of people enjoy small towns like Hastings, but I like big cities better. I'm used to seeing a lot of people. I feel like a quiet environment makes me a little nervous. When you walk down the street and there are no people anywhere and then, all of a sudden, there's a person coming, and I have to think about whether or not I should say hello. I feel obligated to say hello when there's not many people, even to a stranger. It's like two people trapped in an elevator. I don't have this feeling when I am in a big city. I've been outside of Hastings to cities like Lincoln, Omaha, Chicago, New York, and L.A. We talked about moving to a bigger city, but we probably won't do it as of now. His family and business are here and that is why we moved back. Other than it being quiet, I enjoy Hastings, and I'll find things to do.

In my free time I read and take random online classes on Coursera; they offer online classes from many universities all over the world. I go to school for fun, and it helps me get to know America and its culture. I didn't know much about America, other than from what I have learned from school, books, the Internet, and tv shows. It has been fun getting to know it from my own personal experience. Another one of my hobbies is cooking, sometimes we invite friends over and cook for them. I also taught two cooking classes at a church here in town. We cook Chinese food at home, as I find it difficult to find food I like in Hastings. The Chinese food here is different compared to where I am from in China. I've also given a presentation on China at the community college and for the multi-Cultural Association at the YWCA.

Some people are curious and try to understand people like me from other cultural backgrounds. People will ask interesting questions.

I am sometimes surprised by the questions. There's a lot of social pressure in China because of the huge population, and we have to compete for everything. I was once asked if I feel less pressure here. I think there's a lot of financial pressure here to pay your bills and student loans. But I think the pressure here is not a lot compared to that of Chinese students. But I'm not a student here, so I don't know about the real situation. I wouldn't say I could've handled the pressure better than others here. I didn't grow up in this culture, and I'm still learning about it. I think the pressure I had from school makes me realize that I could overcome a lot. It gave me confidence that life is not that difficult.

I'm an atheist. It's very different here than in China. I think people here are more likely to have a Christian background or some other religious background. There are so many churches in Hastings, I'm surprised that there are even more churches than schools. Some people in America try to tell me about their religious beliefs. I don't know if it's a bad thing to be atheist in a country with a Christian culture like America. Maybe it is because of the stereotype that we don't have religious freedom in China, even though that's not the case. When people insist on this stereotype, I don't really want to argue about it. They may be suspicious that I'm just covering it up, even though I am not.

I'm very comfortable talking about religion. But the truth is, religion is just not a big part of our lives. We don't talk about religion all that much in China, but we all respect each other's views. To us, the differences are more about cultural differences rather than religious beliefs. It's a mutual thing that we all agree to disagree. It is just like saying, "they do it this way in this town" or "they do it this way in this country" and we're like, "wow, that's so different than where I'm from." We respect what other people do, even if it is different than what we do. When studying geography and world history in high school, we were taught a little bit about other cultures but not in depth. I find it very interesting to learn about different cultures around the world.

My family does have some religious practices, like praying to our ancestors or offering them a sacrifice. Usually it is a food dish, like fruit or meat. We also go to our ancestors' graves and clean them for the Qingming Festival. These rituals are more culturally religious. I don't actually believe my ancestors are in another place watching over me. When I was a kid, it made more sense and I used to believe that there was an after-life. After people died, I thought they just went to another world and waited in line to come back to life again. But as I grew older, I don't believe that anymore. I think it stopped making sense to me as I learned more about other religions like Islam, Christianity, Hinduism, and

Buddhism in China. As I learned more about these religions, I thought they can't all be true at the same time. I just decided I didn't want to be part of any religion, even though they are very fascinating to me.

I don't associate myself with any political party in America or China. There is a lot going on and I only know a little bit about politics here since I'm new to this country. I read about it, but I don't know this country well enough to form an opinion.

I don't feel like I've ever been treated badly or discriminated against by anyone in Hastings. People don't treat me worse than others, at least not yet. Maybe it's because I don't have to interact with people a lot. Other people of Chinese ethnicity may have different stories when it comes to discrimination. I think some people may be curious about me not being associated with any religion, but I wouldn't consider it discrimination. I think people here are really nice, and I feel understood by others in the community.

The biggest obstacle I have had to overcome since moving to Hastings is understanding the tipping culture. It is weird when I go to restaurants with my friends here. In China, you just pay for your food and that's it. If there's a service fee, the restaurant will print it out on top of your food bill and you don't have to calculate it yourself. I'm not sure how much you should tip a person or at which restaurants you need to tip. That's really confusing. I think the first few months when I went out to get a coffee with a friend I had to ask if I should tip. It's very confusing. Another different thing in Hastings is that people don't hang their clothes outside to dry like we do in China. We hung our clothes outside in China, but we hang our clothes inside above our floor vent here.

I really don't know if there is anything to help increase the Chinese population here. It would be very difficult to live here if they can't speak and read English well. The environment is not very friendly to people who speak other languages like Chinese. I think it would make Chinese people feel more welcome if some people here learned Chinese. I know it is a little impractical with having such a small Chinese population but having some signs in Chinese might also help. I think there are signs in English and Spanish, but there are no signs in other languages. I understand it's not realistic to have every language listed on signs, so I really don't know what a practical way would be to do it.

If I would give some advice on how to change Hastings, I think the city can do more to develop itself. It could then continue to grow and be more beneficial to the residents here. I don't see many business opportunities around town. Maybe it's just me being a business-minded person, but more people would come here for better jobs and income if there were more opportunities. It has the potential to become a bigger and better city in that way. There are some educated people in Hastings. Hastings has both a private and community college. And with other universities in the University of Nebraska system, Hastings should have a lot of educated people living in the area. I just don't know if they are being utilized enough to make the city better, but it has the potential to be a very vibrant place. It's just very quiet here so far.

My name is Zaid. I am from Iraq. I started to know [American] people through the army. My father read all the time and he believed in the Democracy. The Americans came to Iraq to make liberation and my father encouraged me to join the US Army. I intensified my language as much as I could [by myself] with a lot of books. I read a lot. I joined the US Army from 2007 until 2011. [Since] I was working with the US Army, they gave me permission to come here. They call it the SI visa, a Special Immigration visa. They give it just to special guys at high levels because they may do a big favor for the US Army. I'm very happy to come here and meet the old American person here in the United States. That's my life in short.

I was born in Baghdad. I never [went] outside Iraq before. Where I come from is a very beautiful town. It's a very nice place. I finished my elementary school, my middle school, and even my high school back there. For some bad circumstances I stopped. I graduated from the high school, but I didn't go anywhere after. I am not completed after I graduated from

Interviewed by Timothy Herbek

zaid

high school, because I saw there is no benefit. There's no reason to complete it because our country doesn't care about that too much, about the education. That's the only reason.

I had a very big dream to complete my education back there in Iraq, but our system is wrong. They give you a hard time for nothing. My kids came to hate the education system in Iraq, but here in the US they love it. One of my kids took a high level in math, and then everybody clapped for him. My other son put his drawing in the champion newspaper because he draws very well. They encourage them. That's why I like the American education system.

[Now that I am in the US] I'm in the Central Community College. I had to complete my GED. When I was with the US Army, we were talking very well. Since I came here, I found the academic world is very, very hard. I still need to learn some other vocab to develop my academic language. Language actually is very difficult for me, but with education and college it's very easy.

My father came from the farm and then [went] to Baghdad. He struggled. He studied [and] he became an engineer. He is good. My mom came with him from the farm, in a different province, to Baghdad. Everybody [from] a family farm, old families, had many kids. So, I have six sisters and six brothers. We are a very huge family, actually. It's very hard to learn how to control it. My father struggled to grow. He gave us anything we need. I believe that. We pray for him. All of us will pray for him, for God to give him more life. I'm Muslim.

I believe that the leader that is coming, his priority should be no corruption. We suffer from the corruptions of the leaders back home. They are starting to spoil everything, especially the education and the businesses. I like how there isn't a lot of corruption here in the US, especially when it comes to the school systems here in the US.

All the time I am thinking about my future and my kids' futures. I mainly left Iraq to get a better life and better chances in the US, especially in education. The US has a way better school system than back home. I wanted myself and my children to be able to succeed and have the chance to be able to get a full level of high education at all levels. I want to see my children enjoy their childhood and graduate high school and college with a degree and not have to worry about the struggle of trying to find a job when they go into the workforce.

I left Iraq in 2017 for the United States at the age of forty-five with my kids and my wife. The conditions, as you know, were unfortunately really bad in Iraq when I left. The government [was] really broke down. The militia controls the government. [They] control the police. A lot of people are killed, and they are becoming afraid. There is no way to control these bad groups.

[To prepare for coming to the US] we called American government. They had to do a bunch of screening tests to make sure I was a loyal citizen for them to allow into their country. The process was maybe six months for me, as I was in the US Army. They trusted that I was a loyal citizen and that they could trust me to come into the US As you know, a lot of people like me from the Middle East aren't very trusted by the US government, because it isn't a very stable area. [Since] I was a part of the United States Army, they just had to do very hard screening and hard background checks to make sure I was loyal enough to come in. When I actually came in I had to have my papers checked.

When I left for the US, I left a lot of my family back home. Back home all of my brothers and sisters live there still, but they are busy with the war. They are trying to find a way to join me here in the States. My dad is back home. He's an old guy but I want to find a way to bring him here. [That way] he can live the few last years of his life in peace and harmony without all the government struggles back home. I want him to be here with me and happy.

I go there through the IOM organization. They take care [of] you when you apply, when your visa is ready. You call the IOM organization and they arrange the airplane trip for you. They bring your here, to the United States. When you get a job, you pay back the money for the airplane and trip back to those guys, since they helped you with everything.

America is so diverse. They don't care about religion [or] color. They don't care about that. There's no segregation here. It's not an issue because there are so many diverse people. That was very important to me and my decision to move here. [Everyone back home didn't agree with my decision,] especially when I joined the US Army. Some people have a different, foreign idea about the US Young people were told that America was bad, and they had education, so they would believe these ideas. Without education, the mind is weaker. People thought I was stabbing our country in the back. Most people were jealous that I was able to move to the states.

When I came here, I was surprised to see how advanced everything was here compared to back home. There is a huge system with the computer and the internet. I was shocked, even afraid a little bit, but when you are facing a challenge you have to be a man and you have to just face it. You must take a step forward, not a step back.

The main differences between the two cultures are the education. It is very good in the United States. I wish I could have gotten here sooner, when my kids were younger, so they could experience more of that education. When I was young everything was fine in my country. We were like the foreign people, living a good life. That was until 1980. It was fine, but now the war is destroying everything. We were at war with Iran, our neighbor. We have a border with them. The war spoiled everything. The situation in Iraq with the community, the business, the education, and everything is going down because the war. It took the money, the humans, and destroyed anything [in Iraq]. The life in Iraq became changed for the worst.

I was not treated bad in the US when I first came. I stayed in Texas just six month and then I came in Nebraska. [When] I called all the apartment offices about the deposit, they refused to send it to me. They said I didn't pay. But I did pay. I was far away from them at the time, so I cannot judge.

[In the US my expectations] have been met. In the United States if you follow the law, you will be away from the trouble. I believe that. Of course, in any place in the world there [are] good guys and there [are] bad guys. If you stay away from the bad, you will be safe here.

[I am] now working with the *Hastings Tribune* newspaper delivery. I work the night shift. Most of the people need the newspaper in the early morning at the door. That's why I work the night shift. I'm not sure yet, but in the future, I'll be editor. I find that job as an advertisement in the

Hastings newspaper. I said to myself, "That's the perfect time, the night shift, because I don't have time for a day shift." I'm busy with my kids. I had to get them home and to the school. My wife doesn't work. She has no driving license, so that's why.

I'm just reading [in my free time]. I'm just reading and writing and doing math in my home, especially the Khan Academy. I don't want to waste my time. Sometimes I take my kids to the park and sometimes to the YMCA to do exercise. I training my kids [to play] soccer ball. I believe in the future.

[My wife and I] get married in 2001. I have four kids. The biggest two are daughters and two younger sons. My daughter is now fifteen years old, a freshman. The second daughter is thirteen years old, and in eighth grade at Hastings Middle School. Then we have the twin boys. They are nine years old and in third grade. [My wife and I] met back home in Baghdad. It was like love at first look. We talked on the phone every day. I sent my family to her family to ask about marriage. That is our culture. Then we got married.

My family and I love to go to the bigger cities in Nebraska on the weekends and go to museums. We don't just stay home. We like trips to get out of the house. I take my kids fishing all the time just to get them out of the house and out of town. I also like to watch my kids play soccer. I like to help teach them and help them with drills, so they can be the best they can be in what they love.

[The] people [are] very nice. It's very quiet and most people are very helpful. They help you. Especially the education guys are very helpful. When I ask for something they do what they can to help. The people have treated me very nice. I'm a volunteer for after school activities. Most of the guys here are cool, so I have find a way to be part of the community anyway I can. I help this community [by] being a volunteer with the after-school community.

Way of life in Hastings is a very nice environment. It's a very good town, especially if you looking for a town that isn't very busy all the time. Everyone is very quiet and very close even if you live all the way across town. The schools are very close to you, even Walmart is very close. All the shopping marts are close to you. You don't have to drive a long way to get to a place. Everyone here drives very nice, not trying to run you off the road. I went to Michigan with my family, very busy town. I don't like when people drive so fast. Here in Hastings I have never heard a horn, but in Michigan I hear a lot of horns honk and a lot of people yelling at people from car to car.

Hastings is good. The government just needs [to] help businesses. There just aren't a bunch of very big factories. I would like to see the government give our small town an investment to help get more big factories in Hastings to help our town be more advanced like a big city. It needs a project. I like that it is a small and quiet town. I like that I am able to travel quickly and more efficient and only take a few minutes to get to one place or another without having to worry about taking bus or taxi car around town. But in the future, it has [to grow] to become a bigger town.

www.ingramcontent.com/pod-product-compliance
Lightning Source LLC
Chambersburg PA
CBHW051751100526
44591CB00017B/2659